SOUTH EAST SCOTLAND

at Home and Abroad

1800-1850

By
David Dobson

CLEARFIELD

Published for Clearfield Company by
Genealogical Publishing Company
Baltimore, Maryland
2022

ISBN: 9780806359557

THE PEOPLE OF SOUTH EAST SCOTLAND, AT HOME AND ABROAD, 1800-1850

INTRODUCTION

This volume identifies people from the old counties of West Lothian, Mid Lothian, East Lothian, Berwickshire, Roxburghshire, Selkirkshire, and Peeblesshire, now known as Lothian and Borders, of the period 1800 to 1850. The information derives from a wide range of contemporary sources such as court records, newspapers and journals, monumental inscriptions and documents found in archives. The main families traditionally found in the region, which stretches from the Firth of Forth to the border with England, include Home, Lindsay, Elphinstone, Seton, Dundas, Hamilton, Scott, Elliot, and Douglas.

The society and economy of South East Scotland at the time was rural and depended on industries such as farming, fishing, whaling, coal-mining, and forestry. There were several, long established, small burghs in the region, which were either market towns, fishing ports or administrative centres, including Kelso, Dunbar, Melrose, Haddington, Musselburgh, Galashiels, Peebles, Jedburgh, Dalkeith, Linlithgow, Queensferry, Prestonpans, and Selkirk. The River Tweed forms the natural border between Scotland and England, however Berwick-on-Tweed, once one of Scotland's original burghs, is legally in Northumberland, England. The most important town in south east Scotland was, and is, Edinburgh, which has been covered in my book, *The People of Edinburgh and Leith, at Home and Abroad, 1800-1850*.

For those wishing to put their Scottish family history into context the best sources are the Old Statistical Accounts of the 1790s and the New Statistical Accounts compiled between 1832 and 1845. These accounts were produced by parish ministers and covered a wide range of subjects, such as geography, education, history, the economy, agriculture, shipping, population, and religion. These Accounts are available on the website of the National Library of Scotland. Possibly the best collection of local history and family histories can be found in the library of the Scottish Genealogy Society in Edinburgh. Local family history societies include the Borders FHS in Galashiels, the Lothians FHS in Bonnyrigg, and the West Lothian FHS in Bathgate. A useful source on migration from the region to the industrial towns or overseas is Peter Aitchison and Andrew Cassell's *'The Lowland Clearances, Scotland's Silent revolution, 1760-1830'*.

David Dobson, Dundee, Scotland, 2022

REFERENCES

AJ Aberdeen Journal, series

ANY St Andrew's Society of New York

AP St Andrew's Society of Philadelphia

AR Acadian Recorder, series

ARM Madeira Regional Archives, Funchal

AUPC Annals of the United Presbyterian Church

BA Officers of the Bengal Army

BM Blackwood's Magazine, series

CFR Cockburn Family Records

CM Caledonian Magazine, series

DGH Dumfries & Galloway Herald, series

DM Dunfermline Museum

DPCA Dundee, Perth, & Cupar Advertiser, series

EA Edinburgh Advertiser, series

EC Edinburgh Courant, series

EEC Edinburgh Evening Courant, series

ERA Edinburgh Register of Apprentices

F Fasti Ecclesiae Scoticanae

FE Fifeshire Express, series

FH Fife Herald, series

FJ Fife Journal, series

GA Glasgow Advertiser, series

GaGaz. Georgia Gazette, series

GC Glasgow Courier, series

GH Glasgow Herald, series

Gk.Ad. Greenock Advertiser, series

GM Gentleman's Magazine, series

GWS Glasgow & West Scotland Family History Society

HAR History of the Ancient Rydales

HEC Haddington Episcopal Church Records

HJ Halifax Journal, Nova Scotia, series

HPC History of the Presbyterian Church

JSH Journal of Southern History, series

LCL Leith Commercial Lists, series

MAGU Matriculation Album, Glasgow University

MCA Marischal College, Aberdeen

NARA National Archives, Records Administration

NEHGS New England Historic Genealogical Society

NRS National Records of Scotland

OS Oliver Surname on the Scottish Borders

OW Oceans of Wine, [Yale, 2009]

PCC Prerogative Court of Canterbury

PJD People's Journal, Dundee, series

POD Post Office Directory

QM Quebec Mercury, series

S Scotsman, series

Scot.Gen/SG Scottish Genealogist, series

SM Scots Magazine, series

SRA Strathclyde Regional Archives

SSP Records of the Scots Settlers on the River Plate, [Buenos Ayres, 1897]

TNA The National Archives, London

UPC History of the United Presbyterian Church

W The Witness, series

The town of Linlithgow

Linlithgow Castle

Linlithgow church and palace gateway

Linlithgow palace

Cross well - Linlithgow street scene

Haddington High Street

The town of Kelso

Ruins of Melrose Abbey

Hawthronden

Craigmillar Castle

AFFLECK, WILLIAM, born 1807 in Lamancha, Newlands, a sawyer, was accused of discharging a firearm and wounding in Penicuik, Midlothian, in 1832. [NRS.AD14.32.384]

AIKEN, JOHN, a weaver in Yetholm, Roxburghshire, a thief was sentenced in Jedburgh to be transported to the colonies for fourteen years in October 1790. [AJ.2230]

AIKEN, ROBERT, born 1734 in Dalkeith, Midlothian, a publisher in Pennsylvania, died in 1802. [SSA.86]

AIKMAN, ALEXANDER, born 23 June 1755 in Bo'ness, West Lothian, second son of Andrew Aikman and his wife Anne Hunter, emigrated to South Carolina in 1771, a Loyalist who settled in Jamaica in 1778 as a printer and publisher, died at Prospect Pen, St Andrew's, Jamaica, on 6 July 1838. [GM.ns.10.556]

AIRE, ISOBEL, and Son, merchants in Coldstream Berwickshire, in 1794. [Duns Archives, F9.49]

AIR, ROBERT, from Berwick-on-Tweed, married Sarah Justice Musgrove, fourth daughter of Thomas Musgrove in Liverpool, in Egypt on 15 March 1852. [W.317]

AITCHISON, ALEXANDER, born 1832, son of Hugh Aitchison and his wife Isabella, died in the Police Camp, Tolsomairine, New Zealand, on 22 May 1876. [Hutton gravestone, Roxburghshire]

AITCHISON, AMELIA, daughter of John Aitchison in Skerling, Peebles-shire, wife of Reverend John M. McGregor, died in Hammond, USA, on 4 January 1857. [EEC.23006]

AITCHISON, DAVID, son of David Aitchison and his wife Elspeth Fairbairn in Highlaw, Coldingham, Berwickshire, died in Tobago in 1827. [Coldingham Priory gravestone]

AITCHISON, ROBERT, born 1784 in Roxburghshire, a merchant in Charleston, South Carolina, who was naturalised there on 11 December 1813. [NARA.M1183.1]

AIKEN, JOHN, a weaver in Yetholm, Roxburghshire, a thief was sentenced in Jedburgh to be transported to the colonies for fourteen years in October 1790. [AJ.2230]

AIKEN, ROBERT, born 1734 in Dalkeith, Midlothian, a publisher in Pennsylvania, died in 1802. [SSA.86]

AIKMAN, ALEXANDER, born 23 June 1755 in Bo'ness, West Lothian, second son of Andrew Aikman and his wife Anne Hunter, emigrated to South Carolina in 1771, a Loyalist who settled in Jamaica in 1778 as a printer and publisher, died at Prospect Pen, St Andrew's, Jamaica, on 6 July 1838. [GM.ns.10.556]

AIRD, JAMES, born 1797, a carpenter, with his wife, Mary, and one child emigrated from Leith aboard the Symmetry, master William Cochrane, bound for Argentina on 22 May 1825. [SSP.18]

AIRE, ISOBEL, and Son, merchants in Coldstream, Berwickshire, in 1794. [Duns Archives, F9.49]

AIRE, JOHN, son of Lieutenant John Aire RN in Leith, graduated MD from Edinburgh University in 1802, a surgeon of the 31st Regiment of Foot who died in Oporto, Portugal, on 8 September 1809. [SM.71.878]

AIR, ROBERT, from Berwick-on-Tweed, Northumberland, married Sarah Justice Musgrove, fourth daughter of Thomas Musgrove in Liverpool, in Egypt on 15 March 1852. [W.317]

AITCHISON, ALEXANDER, born 1832, son of Hugh Aitchison and his wife Isabella, died in the Police Camp, Tolsomairine, New Zealand, on 22 May 1876. [Hutton gravestone, Roxburghshire]

AITCHISON, AMELIA, daughter of John Aitchison in Skerling, Peebles-shire, wife of Reverend John M. McGregor, died in Hammond, USA, on 4 January 1857. [EEC.23006]

AITCHISON, ANDREW, in Upper Canada, son and heir of Andrew Atchison, an innkeeper in Lauder, in 1854. [NRS.S/H]

AITCHISON, ANNE, in Lauder, sister and heir of Andrew Aitchison in Jackson, USA, in 1854. [NRS.S/H]

AITCHISON, DAVID, son of David Aitchison and his wife Elspeth Fairbairn in Highlaw, Coldingham, Berwickshire, died in Tobago in 1827. [Coldingham Priory gravestone]

AITCHISON, ROBERT, born 1784, a merchant from Roxburghshire, applied to become a citizen of South Carolina on 11 December 1813. [NARA.M1183.1]

AITCHISON, WILLIAM, born 1780 in Hawick, Roxburghshire, a merchant in Charleston, South Carolina, by 1800, died on 17 April 1812, [Old Scots gravestone, Charleston]

AITKEN, ANN, eldest daughter of Robert Aitken a merchant in Dalkeith, Mid Lothian, married Dr William John King from Barbados, in Edinburgh on 26 June 1820. [BM.7.462]

AITKEN, GEORGE, third son of George Aitken portioner of the Bridgend of Dalkeith, Mid Lothian, settled in Fayette, Kentucky, by 1820. [NRS.CS17.1.39/222]

AITKEN, JOHN, a weaver in Dalkeith, Mid Lothian, settled in America by 1820. [NRS.CS17.1.39/222]

AITKEN, JOHN, a clerk of the East Lothian Bank in Dunbar, East Lothian, a process of divorce against his spouse Helen Easton in 1823. [NRS.CC8.6.1874]

AITKEN, MARGARET, daughter of Robert Aitken a wright at Parkend, Dunbar, East Lothian, alleged wife of John Bartholemew, Process of Declarator of Marriage, March 1792. [NRS.CC8.6.879]

AITKEN, PETER, born 1852, died in Boston, Massachusetts, on 28 June 1887. [Torpichen gravestone, West Lothian]

AITKEN, ROBERT, born 1734 in Dalkeith, Mid Lothian, settled in Philadelphia, Pennsylvania, in 1769, died there on 15 July 1802. [AP]

AITKEN, THOMAS, born 1799 in Bo'ness, West Lothian, son of James Aitken a merchant, was educated at Glasgow University in 1818, Rector of Halifax Academy, Nova Scotia, from 1828. [F.7.613]

AITKEN, WILLIAM, a merchant in Dunbar, East Lothian, a Process of Divorce against his spouse Margaret Grant in 1808. [NRS.CC8.6.1326]

ALCORN, ARCHIBALD, born 1852 in Kelso, Roxburghshire, died 1914, husband of Margery McDonald, born 1852, died 1924. [Blackville gravestone, New Brunswick]

ALEXANDER, or SCOTT, HELEN, in Melbourne, Australia, daughter of George Alexander in Jedburgh, Roxburghshire, died on 8 May 1871. [NRS.S/H]

ALEXANDER JOHN, a joiner in Dunbar, East Lothian, was accused of rioting in Dunbar in 1816. [NRS.SC40.54.1.32]

ALLAN, JOHN, born 1791, a labourer from Cockburnspath, Berwickshire, emigrated via Greenock to Ontario in July 1815. [TNA.AO3; CO385.2]

ALLAN, THOMAS, from Tweedside. Peebles, died in New York on 11 December 1826. [BM.21.374]

ALLAN, Mrs THOMAS, from Tweedale, Peebles-shire, died in Hoboken, New York in September 1822. [EEC.1782] [BM.14.373]

ALLANSHAW, JAMES, born 1792 in Berwick-on-Tweed, Northumberland, settled in New Brunswick for 30 years, a merchant and a magistrate, died in St Andrews, N.B., in 1844. [W.5.457]

ALLISTER, CATHERINE, daughter of William Allister in Beveridgewells, died in Greenville, Connecticut, on 9 September 1870. [DP]

AMOS, JOHN, born 1754, tenant in Newbarn, died 1 March 1834, husband of Elizabeth Lawrie, born 1756, died 16 June 1832. [Garvald gravestone, East Lothian]

ANDERSON, ALEXANDER, a farmer in Gloucester Ottawa, Ontario, son and heir of John Anderson, a mason in Selkirk, who died on 10 October 1849. [NRS.S/H]

ANDERSON, ARCHIBALD, born 1765 in East Lothian, a mechanic who died on 8 September 1801. [Old Scots gravestone, Charleston, S.C.]

ANDERSON, DAVID, born 1775, a farmer, with his wife and two children, emigrated via Leith aboard the Symmetry bound for Argentina in 1825. [SSP.18]

ANDERSON, DUNCAN, born 1757 in Stenton, East Lothian, died in 1796. [St James gravestone, Montego Bay, Jamaica]

ANDERSON, ISOBELLA, relict of William Scott in Hawick Shiells, Roxburghshire, heir to her rights at Calla Burn, 1793. [NRS.S/H]

ANDERSON, JAMES, a saddler in Paris, France, son and heir of William Anderson a saddler in Haddington, East Lothian, in 1830. [NRS.S/H]

ANDERSON, JAMES, messenger at arms in Haddington, East Lothian, in 1849. [POD]

ANDERSON, JOHN, born 1810 in Swinton, son of John Anderson, [1785-1869], and his wife Isabella Aitchison, [1783-1835], died in Kingston, Canada West, on 1 February 1859. [Swinton gravestone, Berwickshire]

ANDERSON, JOHN, a librarian in Hotitika, New Zealand, son and heir of Thomas Anderson, a blacksmith in Hawick, Roxburghshire, who died on 21 March 1873. [NRS.S/H]

ANDERSON, MARGARET, daughter of John Anderson of Gladswood, Berwickshire, married Captain G. Walter Story, in Frankfort, Germany, in 1835. [GA.5084]

ANDERSON, ROBERT, born 1747 in Tranent, East Lothian, emigrated to Jamaica in May 1778, died at Flower Hill, St James, Jamaica, on 9 August 1796. [Montego Bay gravestone, Jamaica]

ANDERSON, ROBERT, in New York, son and heir of Robert Anderson, a fruit merchant in Corstorphine, Mid Lothian, who died on 13 September 1872. [NRS.S/H]

ANDERSON, THOMAS, born 1738, son of John Anderson and his wife Jean Hastie, settled in Westmoreland, Jamaica, died on 12 February 1796. [Kirkliston gravestone, West Lothian]

ANDERSON, THOMAS BROWN, a merchant in Montreal, Quebec, son of Peter Anderson, a merchant died 1820, and his wife Magdalene Anderson. [Buccleugh gravestone, Roxburghshire]

ANDERSON, THOMAS, a blacksmith in Hawick, Roxburghshire, died on 21 March 1873, father of John Anderson a librarian in Hotika, New Zealand. [NRS.S/H]

ANNAN, ROBERT, son of John Annan a locksmith in Queensferry, West Lothian, was apprenticed to Ebenezer Annan, a locksmith in Edinburgh, for six years on 6 October 1791. [ERA]

ANTHONY, JAMES, a vintner in Linlithgow, West Lothian, in 1823. [NRS.B48.16.6.4]

ARBUCKLE, HUGH, a merchant and shipowner in Queensferry, West Lothian, master of the Margaret of Queensferry trading with Norway and with Memel, day books 1802-1807. [NRS.CS96.4143-4165]

ARCHIBALD, THOMAS, a brewer in Dalkeith, Mid Lothian, a bond in 1822. [NRS.GD81.313]

ARMSTRONG, GEORGE, born 1788 in Roxburghshire, emigrated to America in 1819, settled in Ovid, New York. [SG.32.3]

ARMSTRONG, THOMAS, born in Roxburghshire, emigrated to America in 1819, settled in Ovid, New York. [SG.32.3]

ARMSTRONG, WILLIAM, born in Roxburghshire, emigrated to America in 1819, settled in Ovid, New York. [SG.32.3]

ARNEIL, ANDREW, born 1817, died in February 1852, husband of Elizabeth Lawton, born 1814, died on 11 July 1879. [Kelso gravestone, Roxburghshire]

ARNOTT, ANDREW, in Little York, Pennsylvania, grandson of Reverend Andrew Arnott in Midlem, appointed his uncle Andrew Arnott in Millrighall, Roxburghshire, and Thomas Usher in Courthill, Roxburghshire, as his attornies in 1812. [NRS.RD5.53.27]

ARNOT, LAMONT, a farmer in MacNab, Bathurst, Canada, heir to his grandfather John Arnot in Prestonpans later in Musselburgh, Mid Lothian, in 1853. [NRS.S/H]

ASHTON, EDWARD, in California, heir to William Weatherhead, a physician in Coldstream, Berwickshire, in 1857. [NRS.S/H]

ASTLEY, JOSEPH, a chemistry manufacturer in Portobello, Mid Lothian, and in Bo'ness, West Lothian, sederunt books, 1820-1826. [NRS.CS96.3580/3590]

ASTLEY, THOMAS, a chemist in Musselburgh, Mid Lothian, brother of Charles Joseph Astley a merchant in Pernambuco, Brazil, in 1851. [NRS.S/H]

AULD, JANET, born 1775 in Whitburn, West Lothian, second wife of Reverend James McGregor, died 10 July 1851, buried at Iron Bridge, New Glasgow, Nova Scotia. [SG]

BAILLIE, GEORGE, formerly a merchant in Georgia, later in Coats, Haddington, East Lothian, a bond dated 2 October 1794. [NRS.RD3.279.116]; Loyalist claims 1784-1787. [TNA.AO12.74.101, etc]

BAILLIE, GEORGE, of Jerviswood, a deed, registered on 21 December 1841. [NRS.RD29.3.23]

BAIN, ELIZABETH, daughter of Thomas Bain in Loanhead, Mid Lothian, married Reuben Shepherd in Brooklyn, New York, on 1 May 1857. [S]

BAIN, WILLIAM E., in Cherokee Flat, California, son and heir of Edward Bain, a labourer in Greenlaw, Berwickshire, who died on 25 January 1868. [NRS.S/H]

BAIRD, Sir JAMES, of Saughtonhall, Mid Lothian, father of Captain William Baird who died in Boulogne-sur-mere, France, on 20 May 1823. [SM.86.776]

BAIRD, JOHN, in Sydney, New South Wales, Australia, son and heir of Thomas Baird, a surgeon in Linlithgow, West Lothian, who died on 1 December 1825. [NRS.S/H]

BAIRD, Reverend JOHN, and his wife Elizabeth Hughes, were parents of James Oliver Baird, born 26 March 1853, who died in Hanover, Germany on 25 January 1872. [F.2.96]

BAIRD, MARGARET HOME, of Coldingham, Berwickshire, testament, 1796, Comm. Lauder. [NRS]

BAIRD, RICHARD FREDERICK, youngest son of Sir James Gardiner Baird of Saughtonhall, Mid Lothian, died in Bermuda on 15 June 1819. [S.131.19]

BAIRD, Captain WILLIAM, son of Sir James Baird of Saughtonhall, Mid Lothian, died in Boulogne-sur-Mer, France, on 20 May 1823. [SM.86.776]

BAIRNSFATHER, WILLIAM, son of Peter Bairnsfather tenant in Harperdean, died in Jamaica in 1791, , a writer there, his testament refers to William Veitch, a watchmaker in Haddington, also John Craw, a writer in Haddington, East Lothian, in 1794. [NRS.CC8.8.129]

BALFOUR, JAMES, in Whittinghame, East Lothian, was the victim of poaching in 1827. [NRS.AD14.27.29]

BALFOUR, JAMES MAITLAND, of Whittinghame, Berwickshire, died and was buried in Funchal, Madeira, in 1856. [NRS.GD33.1.316; GD314.56]

BALFOUR, JOHN, born 25 September 1798 in Bowden, Roxburghshire, son of Reverend William Balfour and his wife Mary Mein, died in Boston, Massachusetts, on 15 August 1844. [F.2.172]

BALL, GEORGE, born 1795, son of Robert Ball and his wife Jane, died in Tobago on 17 February 1822. [Ayton gravestone, Berwickshire]

BALLANTYNE, JAMES BURN, in Fort Clark, Texas, heir to Thomas Vair, a merchant in Kelso, Roxburghshire, who died on 15 October 1830. [NRS.S/H]

BALLANTYNE, JAMES, of Holylee, born 22 May1789, died on 30 March 1870, husband of Anne Henderson, born in April 1797, died on 11 December 1858. [Innerleithen gravestone, Peebles-shire]

BALMER, ROBERT, a merchant in Montreal, Quebec, son and heir of Richard Balmer, a mason in Cessford, Roxburghshire, who died on 11 April 1849. [NRS.S/H]

BANKS, ARCHIBALD, born 1808, from Longniddry, East Lothian, died in Sunnyside, Brisbane, Queensland, Australia, on 1 January 1885. [S.12992]

BANKS, JAMES, a weaver in Belhaven, East Lothian, was accused of rioting in Dunbar, East Lothian, in 1816. [NRS.SC40.54.1.31]

BAPTIE, MARGARET, born in Roxburghshire, died in Montreal, Quebec, on 24 March 1857. [EEC.21078]

BARCLAY, HENRY, from Dunbar, East Lothian, died at the Hermitage, Jamaica, on 3 May 1860. [DC.23505]

BARR, JOHN, son of William Barr, [1751-1787], died in Tobago on 22 September 1808. [Eyemouth gravestone, Berwickshire]

BARSTOW, JANE, in Kelso, Roxburghshire, letter, 1807 to 1837. [NRS.GD113.5.98]

BATHGATE, ANDREW, born 1805, a labourer in North Berwick, East Lothian, was accused of theft, housebreaking, and fire-raising in Haddington, East Lothian, in 1849. [NRS.AD14.49.104]

BARTHOLEMEW, ANNA, daughter of George Bartholemew a merchant in Linlithgow, West Lothian, married Ralph Bowie, a counsellor at law in Philadelphia, Pennsylvania, in Edinburgh on 15 July 1788. [Edinburgh Marriage Register]

BARTHOLEMEW, GEORGE, a merchant in Linlithgow, West Lothian, dead by 1805. [NRS.S/H]

BARTHOLEMEW, JAMES, , was accused of culpable and furious driving a cart in Currie, Mid Lothian, in 1825. [NRS.AD14.25.36]

BARTLEMAN, ARCHIBALD, father of Alexander Bartleman, born 1853, died in Dunedin, Otago, New Zealand, on 4 January 1903. [West Linton gravestone, Peebles-shire]

BAXTER, HARRIET, born 27 November 1814 in Lilliesleaf, Roxburghshire, daughter of Reverend David Baxter and his wife Ann Campbell, married Joseph French a chemist in Australia, died 15 July 1890. [F.2.183]

BAXTER, HELEN FRANCES, born in Lilliesleaf, Roxburghshire, daughter of Reverend David Baxter and his wife Ann Campbell, married E. N. Houston a surgeon in Australia, died 17 October 1902. [F.2.183]

BAXTER, JEMIMA NICOLINA, born 20 July 1814 in Lilliesleaf, Roxburghshire, daughter of Reverend David Baxter and his wife Ann Campbell, married William King, a minister in Nelson, Ontario, in Hamilton, Canada West on 15 September 1853, she died in 1887. [F.2.183] [EEC.22494]

BAYNE, GEORGE, a mason in Dunbar, East Lothian, later with the Leith Gas Works, versus his spouse Katherine Stewart, a Process of Divorce in 1805. [NRS.CC8.6.1239]

BEGARNIE, MARGARET, daughter of James Begarnie a shoemaker in Dunbar, East Lothian, a process of divorce against her husband Robert Johnstone, a gentleman's servant in Edinburgh, in 1813. [NRS.CC8.6.1509]

BEGBIE, ELIZABETH, wife of Captain Yarrel in Carolina, heir to her grand-uncle William Begbie of Gifford Vale, East Lothian in 1827. [NRS.S/H]

BEGBIE, THOMAS, in Williamstown, North Carolina, heir to his grand-uncle William Begbie of Gifford Vale, East Lothian in 1827. [NRS.S/H]

BEGG DAVID, from Musselburgh, Mid Lothian, emigrated to Poyais, Central America, died in Belize in 1823. [EEC.17520]

BELL, GEORGE, born 1795, son of Robert Bell and his wife Jane Hamilton in Nethermyres Mill, Ayton, Berwickshire, died in Tobago on 17 February 1822. [Ayton gravestone]

BELL, GEORGE, a teacher in Newcastle, son and heir of Ninian Bell a mason in Jedburgh, Roxburghshire, 1843. [NRS.S/H]

BELL, JAMES, born 1809, son of David Bell, [1778-1859], and his wife Elizabeth Hunter, [1780-1837], died in New York on 25 August 1859, interred in Greenwood Cemetery, N.Y. [Duns gravestone, Berwickshire]

BELL, JANE, wife of Stephenson Haig in New York, niece and heir of William Bell, a roadman in Duns, Berwickshire, who died on 29 September 1871. [NRS.S/H]

BELL, or WILSON, JANET, in Brooklyn, New York, niece and heir of William Bell, a roadman in Duns, Berwickshire, who died on 29 September 1871. [NRS.S/H]

BELL, PETER, a smith at Pitcox, East Lothian, father of Thomas Bell who died in Buenos Ayres, Argentina, on 18 May 1863. [S.2516]

BELL, WILLIAM, formerly a merchant in Charleston, South Carolina, now in St Andrew's parish, married Isobella Dempster, in Edinburgh on 27 July 1815. [EMR]

BELL, WILLIAM, born 1800, son of John Bell [1768-1830], and his wife Mary Marshall, [1778-1857], died in America on 24 October 1830. [Cockburnspath gravestone, Berwickshire]

BELL, WILLIAM, in Niagara, grandson and heir of Robert Renwick, the Deacon of the Wrights in Jedburgh, Roxburghshire, in 1842. [NRS.S/H]

BENNET, ANDREW, a cabinetmaker in Coldstream, Berwickshire, born 1764, died on 29 April 1836, husband of Margaret Grieve, born 1768, died on 11 August 1801. [Eccles gravestone, Berwickshire]

BENNIE, JOHN, born 1796 probably son of James Bennie a merchant in Haddington, East Lothian, was educated at Glasgow University, a missionary to Kaffraria, South Africa, in 1821, then a minister from 1850 until his death on 9 February 1869. [F.7.560]

BENTLEY, ANTONIA, born 1781, relict of Paul Weston, MD, in Charleston, South Carolina, died in Portobello, Mid Lothian, on 16 December 1857. [Greyfriars gravestone, Edinburgh]

BERTHAM, ALEXANDER, born 1795 in Cranshaws, Berwickshire, son of John Bertram, died in Augusta, Georgia, on 27 November 1827. [Georgia Courier, 29.11.1827] [EA.6695.63]

BERTRAM, JAMES, born 1849, son of Peter Bertram in Bellmount, [1819-1869], and his wife Jessie Stewart, [1829-1908], died in Invercargill, New Zealand, on 7 October 1899. [Eccles gravestone, Berwickshire]

BERTRAM, PETER, son of Peter Bertram a tidewaiter in North Berwick, East Lothian, was apprenticed to Henry Hardie, a baker in Edinburgh, for seven years in May 1797. [ERA]

BERTRAM, WILLIAM, a Major in the Service of the East India Company, son of William Bertram of Nisbet, Berwickshire, 1830. [NRS.S/H]

BEVERIDGE, JOHN, born 1846, third son of Reverend J. G. Beveridge in Inveresk, East Lothian, was killed by Indians near Bahia Blanca, Argentina, on 23 October 1870. [S.8647]

BIGGAR, ROBERT, born 1747, died at Shiplaw, on 21 November 1808. [Eddleston gravestone, Peebles-shire]

BINNEY, ARCHIBALD, born in Portobello, Mid Lothian, in 1763, a typefounder in Philadelphia, Pennsylvania, by 1796, died in 1838. [SSA.86],

BISHOP, JOHN, a merchant in Dalkeith, Mid Lothian, father of William Tyrie Bishop, born 1852, died at sea on voyage home from Bombay, India, on 6 August 1884. [S.12827]

BISHOP, ROBERT HAMILTON, born 26 July 1771 in Longridge, Whitburn, West Lothian, was educated at Edinburgh University in 1798, emigrated to America in 1802, a clergyman and academic at Oxford University, Miami, Ohio, died 29 April 1855. [UPC]

BLACK, AGNES, relict of Thomas Weatherly tenant in Leehouses, died 5 November 1825. [Cockburnspath gravestone]

BLACK, DAVID, a Lieutenant of the 26th Regiment of Foot, died in Peebles on 17 August 1822. [SM.90.520]

BLACK, Reverend PATRICK, youngest son of Reverend Alexander Black in Musselburgh, Mid Lothian, died in Worcester, Cape of Good Hope, South Africa, on 31 January 1847. [AJ.5184]

BLACKADDER, JOHN, a tenant in Edrom, Berwickshire, testament, 1795, Comm. Lauder. [NRS]

BLACKBURN, HUGH, in Boston, Massachusetts, son of the late Bazil Blackburn of Prestonpans, East Lothian, subscribed to a deed in Boston, appointing William Goddard, a merchant in Leith as his attorney, on 8 May 1807. [NRS.RD3.317.299]

BLACKWOOD, W., agent of the British Linen Company in Peebles in 1849. [POD]

BLAIKIE, ANDREW, an engineer in USA, nephew and heir of Francis Blaikie, in St Helens, Roxburghshire, who died on 17 August 1857. [NRS.S/H]

BLAIR, ANN, an innkeeper in North Berwick, East Lothian, widow of Robert Cramond, a mason in Eyemouth, Dunbar, and Port Seton, versus Helen Dunbar in North Berwick, 1839. [NRS.SC40.11.7.13.17]

BLAIR, THOMAS, a mason in Tranent, East Lothian, in 1790. [NRS.JO2.6.3.1.22]

BLAIR, THOMAS, a farmer in Hoprig Mains, East Lothian, father of George Blair who married Margaret Drysdale, daughter of R. P. Drysdale the Mayor of Georgetown, Demerara, and widow of Reverend J. E. Gummer, in Georgetown on 10 August 1881. [S.11909]

BLAKE, Reverend JAMES L., and his wife Janette Bryce, in Stobo, Peebles-shire, were parents of George Alexander Bryce Blake born 30 January 1855, a merchant in America. [F.2.24]

BLAKE, WILLIAM, a farmer, died in Inkbonny, died in November 1856, husband of Helen Pringle, born 1786, died on 1 July 1856. [Eddleston gravestone, Peebles-shire]

BLAKIE, JANE, born 1736, married William Spiden a merchant in Bowden, Roxburghshire, died in Kentucky in 1819. [Bewlie gravestone, Selkirkshire]

BLEAKIE, ROBERT, a butcher and spirit dealer in Dalkeith, Mid Lothian, 1825. [NRS.CS223.Seqn.131/72]

BOGUE, GEORGE, born 1795, son of William Bogue and his wife Elizabeth Murray in Coldingham, Berwickshire, a surgeon who died in Jamaica on 5 September 1817. [Coldingham gravestone]

BOGUE, JOHN, of Prestonhaugh, testament, 1790, Comm. Lauder. [NRS]

BOIG, WILLIAM WHITSON, a master mariner and feuar in Eyemouth, Berwickshire, a sasine, 1848. [NRS.GD267.26.34.671]

BOOKLES, ROBERT, born 1780, tenant in Caldra, died 21 July 1857, husband of Mary Lillie, born 1784, died 10 September 1803. [Fogo gravestone, Berwickshire]

BORTHWICK, ADAM, a shepherd in South Australia, son and heir of Thomas Borthwick a shepherd in Tweedsmuir, Roxburghshire, 1852. [NRS.S/H]

BORTHWICK, GEORGE, born 1738, a merchant and magistrate of Jedburgh, Roxburghshire, died there on 17 September 1822. [SM.90.632]

BORTHWICK, WILLIAM, manager or cashier of the East Lothian Banking Company, absconded to America in 1822. [NRS.GD304][NRS.CS231.Sed.Bk.2/1]

BOSTON, CHRISTINA, born 1750, daughter of Reverend Thomas Boston in Jedburgh, Roxburghshire, and grand-daughter of Reverend Thomas Boston, in Ettrick, Selkirkshire, wife of Tucker Harris, MD, died in Charleston, South Carolina, on 10 March 1818. [BM.3.364]

BOSTON, ROBERT, born 1779 in Kelso, Roxburghshire, a slater in New York from 1806 until 1813, was naturalised there on 17 April 1811, died on 11 December 1813. [ANY]

BOWHILL, THOMAS, in Ayton, Berwickshire, father of John Bowhill who married Amelia Ejarabido in Passo de los Torros, Costa del Rio Negra, Uruguay, on 20 September 1882. [S.12299]

BOWIE, ANNA, ANDREW, and JOHN, children of the late Ralph Bowie in York, Pennsylvania, and his wife Ann Batholemew, daughter of George Bartholemew, a merchant in Linlithgow, West Lothian, and their attorney Alexander Pitcairn, a merchant in Edinburgh, a deed in 1785, witnessed by Robert Paul and David Pitcairn, clerks to Pitcairn and Scott insurance brokers in Edinburgh. [NRS.RD3.305.1153]

BOWIE, ANN ANDREW, daughter of Ralph Bowie in America, grand-daughter and heir of George Bartholemew, a merchant in Linlithgow, West Lothian, in 1805. [NRS.S/H]

BOWIE, JOHN, a carpenter from Dalhousie, Mid Lothian, died in Georgia on 17 September 1801. [Georgia Gazette: 24.9.1801]

BOYD, JOHN, First Lieutenant of the Royal Linlithgow Volunteers, was admitted as a burgess and guilds-brother of Dunfermline, Fife, on 15 August 1804. [DM]

BOYD, ROBERT, a sailor in Bo'ness, West Lothian, 1795. [NRS.S/H]

BRAND, ANDREW, lately in Nevis, died in East Linton, East Lothian, on 31 March 1820. [AJ.3771]

BREATCLIFF, BENJAMIN, in Bathgate, West Lothian, was found guilty of poaching in 1825. [NRS.B48.16.6.6]

BREMNER, THOMAS, a ship's carpenter in Philadelphia, Pennsylvania, son and heir of George Bremner, a feuar in Greenlaw, Berwickshire, in 1799. [NRS.S/H]

BRIDGES, ROBERT, an engineer and millwright in North Berwick, East Lothian, sequestration, 1849. [NRS.CS280.11.8]

BRIGGS, ALEXANDER, eldest son of Alexander Briggs in Dalkeith, Mid Lothian, a merchant in Bridgetown, Barbados, died in Demerara in January 1830. [BM.27.965] [S.1057]

BRIGGS, ALEXANDER, a wine merchant in Dalkeith, Mid Lothian, father of Charles Selkrig Briggs, born 1811 and died in Demerara on 18 January 1832. [EEC.18775][GkAd.3824]

BRIGGS, DAVID, younger brother of Alexander Briggs a wine merchant in Dalkeith, Mid Lothian, died in New York in 1796. [SM.58.650]

BRIGGS, JANE, youngest daughter of George Briggs, a grate and stone manufacturer in Haddington, East Lothian, married John Wright, in Rio de Janeiro, Brazil, on 10 September 1873. [S.9435]

BROAD, JOHN, a farmer from Redfordgreen, Peebles-shire], with Isobel his wife, and six children, emigrated via Greenock to Canada in 1815. [TNA.CO385.2]

BROADWOOD, THOMAS, of Fulfordlees, born 1779, died 11 November 1835, husband of Catherine Sligh, born 26 February 1779, died on 11 April 1853. [Cockburnspath gravestone, Berwickshire]

BROCKIE, JOHN, born 1787, tenant in Belville, died 22 January 1847. [Eccles gravestone, Berwickshire]

BRODIE, ALEXANDER, son of Thomas Brodie and his wife Jean Middlemiss, [1781-1814], settled in Baltimore, Maryland. [Ladykirk gravestone, Berwickshire]

BRODIE, ALEXANDER, in Morphett Vale, South Australia, a sasine 1863, North Berwick, East Lothian. [NRS.R.S.North Berwick,4/111]d

BRODIE, GEORGE, born 1814 in Meggatdale, Selkirkshire, emigrated to America in 1846, settled in New York, died there on 2 May 1866. [ANY]

BRODIE, JAMES, born 1804 in Selkirkshire, a distiller who emigrated via Greenock to America, was naturalised in New York on 14 May 1828. [NARA]

BRODIE, JOHN, son of Thomas Brodie and his wife Jean Middlemiss, [1781-1814], settled in Baltimore, Maryland. [Ladykirk gravestone, Berwickshire]

BRODIE, WILLIAM, eldest son of William Brodie in Selkirk, died in New York on 13 August 1825. [S.609.719]

BROMFIELD, ROBERT, born on 14 March 1846, in Sprouston, Roxburghshire, son of Reverend Robert Bromfield and his wife Mary Weatherstone, a sheep farmer in Queensland, Australia, died 3 January 1888. [F.2.91]

BROMFIELD, Colonel STEPHEN, of Hassington Mains, born 1740, died 31 May 1823. [Eccles gravestone, Berwickshire]

BROMFIELD, THOMAS, born on 20 October 1849, son of Reverend Robert Bromfield and his wife Mary Weatherstone, a sheep farmer in Queensland, Australia, died 3 January 1888. [F.2.91]

BROTHERSTONE, ROBERT, in Paspebiac, Gaspe, Quebec, heir to his great granduncle William Brotherstone in Peebles, in 1841. [NRS.S/H]

BROWN, Dr ALEXANDER, born 1819, son of David Brown in Roseland Cottage, Linlithgow, West Lothian, died in Chillan, Chile, on 30 October 1874. [S.9796]

BROWN, DAVID, a merchant in New York, heir to his grandfather George Dobie, a cordiner in Selkirk, in 1826. [NRS.S/H]

BROWN, DAVID, eldest son of ....Brown a surveyor in Kelso, Roxburghshire, died in Chillan, Chile, on 26 July 1869. [S.8164]

BROWN, EDWARD, a millwright in Buffalo, New York, heir to his grandfather Edward Brown, a wright in Innerwick, East Lothian, who died on 6 November 1836, 17 October 1889. [NRS.S/H]; he died in Manwell City, USA, on 13 March 1874. [EC.27924]

BROWN, GEORGE, in Selkirk, brother and heir of David Brown, a merchant in New York, in 1837. [NRS.S/H]

BROWN, GUSTAVUS, MD, in St Mary's County, Maryland, eldest son of Richard Brown of Charles County, Maryland, eldest son of Gustavus Brown of Mainside, Roxburghshire, MD, heir to the said Gustavus Brown his grandfather, 22 April 1793. [NRS.S/H]

BROWN, JAMES, son of Patrick Brown a farmer at Carleverick, Tranent, East Lothian, was apprenticed to Josiah Maxton, a saddler and beltmaker in Edinburgh, for six years, on 6 July 1792. [ERA]

BROWN, JAMES, from Peebles, later in the USA, a sasine, 8 May 1833. [NRS.RS.Edinburgh.42.95]

BROWN, JAMES, [1825-1892], husband of Mary Spark, [1829-1899], parents of James Brown, born 1865, died in Boston, Massachusetts, on 15 June 1888. [Earlston gravestone, Berwickshire]

BROWN, JANET, born 1785 in Roxburghshire, emigrated aboard the Brilliant bound for East Cape Colony, South Africa, in 1820, settled on the Baviaans River, [Scot.Gen.30.1.32]

BROWN, JOHN, a baker in Kelso, Roxburghshire, son and heir of Robert Brown a baker in Kelso, 1843. [NRS.S/H]

BROWN, ROBERT, a maltman in Dunbar, East Lothian, was accused of rioting in Dunbar in 1816. [NRS.SC40.54.1.32]

BROWN, Mrs SUSANNAH. In Somerset, St Mary's County, Maryland, widow of Dr Gustavus Brown late of Charles County, Maryland, who died in 1801, disposed of the lands of Mainside, Roxburghshire. [NRS.RD5.100.582]

BROWN, SUSAN, wife of Walter Mitchell a shoemaker in Linlithgow, West Lothian, was accused of stealing cabbages in 1825. [NRS.B48.16.6.6]

BROWN, THOMAS, Quartermaster of the Royal Linlithgow Volunteers, was admitted as a burgess and guilds-brother of Dunfermline, Fife, on 15 August 1804. [DM]

BROWN, WILLIAM, son of John Brown the minister of the Associate Congregation in Haddington, East Lothian, was apprenticed to Adam Freer, a merchant in Edinburgh, for five years, on 24 March 1795. [ERA]

BROWN, WILLIAM, in Buffalo, New York, son and heir of William Brown, a farm servant in Penicuik, Mid Lothian, died on 27 September 1856. [NRS.S/H]

BRUCE, ALEXANDER, son of Alexander Bruce a surgeon in Musselburgh, Mid Lothian, was apprenticed to Francis Allan, a wright in Edinburgh, for six years, on 8 October 1800. [ERA]

BRUCE, CHARLES, from Musselburgh, Mid Lothian, died at Rio Bueno, Jamaica, on 18 July 1819. [S.144.19] [EA][AJ.3746]

BRUCE, GEORGE, son of Alexander Bruce a surgeon in Musselburgh, Mid Lothian, was apprenticed to James Latta, a surgeon apothecary in Edinburgh, for five years, on 5 February 1800. [ERA]

BRUCE, JAMES, born 22 June 1772, a shoemaker in Kelso, Roxburghshire, died on 4 November 1856, husband of Jane Hilton, born 21 December 1774, died on 15 November 1849, parents of Mrs Barbara Bruce or Dryden in New York, and of James Bruce, born 31 December 1803, died 15 May 1854 in Troy, N.Y. [Kelso gravestone]

BRUCE, Mrs SELKRIG, widow of Robert Dods of Prora, East Lothian, died in New Windsor, Maryland, on 24 April 1825. [EA.6423.383][EEC.17748]

BRUNTON, WILLIAM, born 1766 in Newbattle, Mid Lothian, emigrated to Canada in 1820, a minister in Quebec from 1820 to his death on 12 August 1839. [F.7.628]

BRYCE, DAVID, from Jamaica, died in Musselburgh, Mid Lothian, on 18 February 1798. [AJ.2618]

BRYCE, JAMES, a farmer in West Calder, Mid Lothian, with Jane his wife and six children, emigrated via Greenock to Canada in 1815. [TNA.CO385.2]

BRYCE, or SMITH, JANET, in America, nephew and heir of John Lyon, in Society, Hopetoun House, West Lothian, in 1833. [NRS.S/H]

BRYCE, JOHN, born 1800 in West Calder, Mid Lothian, died at the North River, Chatham, Quebec, on 19 January 1885. [S.12974]

BRYCE, PETER, born 1800 in West Calder, West Lothian, died at North River, Chatham, Quebec, on 19 January 1885. [S.12974]

BRYCE, WILLIAM, born 1782 in Mid Calder, West Lothian, a saddler in New York, died there on 27 May 1830. [ANY]

BRYDEN, JAMES, an assistant staff surgeon, son of James Bryden a surgeon in Peebles, died on Turk's Island, Bahamas, on 12 July 1832. [EEC.18865]

BRYDEN, WILLIAM, son of Adam Bryden, [1766-1850], and his wife Margaret Armstrong, [1773-1842], died in South Australia. [St Mary's, Selkirk, gravestone]

BUCHAN, JAMES, born 3 September 1812 in Mains of Harelaw, Linton, Roxburghshire, emigrated via Leith to Montreal, Quebec, in 1833, settled in New York in 1835, died there on 29 April 1887. [ANY]

BUCHAN-HEPBURN, JOHN GEORGE, born 24 September 1841, eldest son of Sir Thomas Buchan-Hepburn of Smeaton-Hepburn, died in Pinos Altos, Chihuahua, Mexico, on 21 January 1883. [Preston Kirk gravestone, East Lothian]

BUCHANAN, JAMES, born 1821, son of James Buchanan, an Excise officer, and his wife Janet Redpath, died in Tobago on 4 December 1844. [Spott gravestone, East Lothian]

BUCHANAN, JOHN, born 1767, son of Reverend John Buchanan, [1708-1785], a surgeon who died in Jamaica on 16 March 1798. [Foulden gravestone, Berwickshire]

BUCKHAM, JOHN, of Bush, heir to his father John Buckham a tenant in Bedrule, Roxburghshire, 14 October 1791. [NRS.S/H]

BUIST, DAVID, born 1848, son of Mathew Buist in Tyningham, East Lothian, died in South America on 6 February 1883. [S.12331]

BUCKLES, GEORGE, a shoemaker in North Berwick, East Lothian, and Andrew Thomson, a butcher there, signed a bond of caution to that would not harm Peter Law in East Fenton, 1800. [NRS.CS27.1.3.52]

BUNZIE, WILLIAM, a weaver and portioner of Newstead, Roxburghshire, settled in the Jignor Valley, Westmore County, Pennsylvania, by 1799. [NRS.CS17.1.18/377]

BURD, Colonel JAMES, born 10 March 1726 in Ormiston, East Lothian, son of Edward Burd and his wife June Haliburton, emigrated to Philadelphia, Pennsylvania, fought in the French and Indians War, died 9 October 1793, buried in Middletown, Douglas County, Pennsylvania. [AP]

BURGESS, JAMES, born 1763 in Linlithgow, West Lothian, settled in Charleston, South Carolina, in 1788, died 20 November 1805. [St Michael's gravestone, Charleston]

BURGESS, THOMAS, a boatbuilder from Slateford, Mid Lothian, emigrated to Poyais, Central America, died in 1823. [EEC.17520]

BURN, DAVID, late a merchant in Fisherrow, Mid Lothian, died in Cherokee, Hamilton, Upper Canada, on 2 March 1840. [EEC.20045]

BURN, GEORGE PERCY, born 10 November 1773, son of Reverend William Burn and his wife Margaret Ogle in Roxburghshire, died in Dominica in 1800. [F.2.133]

BURNETT, JAMES, an attorney at law, eldest son of James Burnett of Barns, died in Georgetown, Demerara, on 6 December 1836. [Manor gravestone, Peebles-shire] [AJ.4647]

BURNET, WILLIAM, of Viewfield, Dunbar, East Lothian, married Mary Mercier, daughter of Major Mercier of the island of Jersey, at Swinton House, on 15 October 1822. [SM.90.631]

BURNS, ALEXANDER, second son of Alexander Burns in Grangemouth, West Lothian, married Sarah Gairns, youngest daughter of Andrew Gairns from Cupar, Fife, in Chicago, Illinois, in May 1859. [FH]

BURN, DAVID, a merchant from Fisherrow, Mid Lothian, died in Cherokee, Hamilton, Upper Canada, on 2 March 1840. [EEC.20045]

CAIRNS, EMILY REBECCA, in Birgham, Roxburghshire, niece and heir of William Cairns of Torr, a merchant in New York, who died on 7 October 1860. [NRS.S/H]

CAIRNS, MARY, wife of T. Gilman, a druggist in Birgham, Roxburghshire, niece and heir of William Cairns of Torr, a merchant in New York, who died on 7 October 1860. [NRS.S/H]

CALDER, ADAM, in Belhaven, East Lothian, father of Adam Calder who died in Pergamino, Argentina, in 1879. [S.11410]

CALDWELL, JOHN, born 1798 in Penicuik, Mid Lothian, a machinist in Charleston, South Carolina, was naturalised on 7 April 1847. [NARA.M1183.1]

CALLANDER, JOHN, in Newbigging, Innerwick, East Lothian, a process of scandal against Henry Mason, a tenant in Little Pinkerton, Dunbar, East Lothian, in 1812. [NRS.CC8.6.1489]

CAMERON, ALEXANDER, son of John Cameron in Whitehall, [1760-1836], and his wife Janet Paxton, [1767-1851], died at Ardoise Hill, Nova Scotia, on 1 July 1866. [Chirnside gravestone, Berwickshire]

CAMERON, DONALD, a prisoner in Linlithgow, West Lothian, was accused of prison breaking, in 1820. [NRS.AD14.20.258]

CAMPBELL, ALEXANDER, born 1736 in Trudernish, Islay, late of Tobago, died in Musselburgh, Mid Lothian, on 14 December 1825. [Grayfriars gravestone]

CAMPBELL, GEORGE, eldest son of Reverend Dr Campbell in Ancrum, Roxburghshire, died in Jamaica in 1817. [S.I.42]

CANT, JAMES, son of John Cant a craftsman in Linlithgow, West Lothian, was educated at Glasgow University in 1814, emigrated to America. [MAGU][UPC]

CARMICHAEL, THOMAS, a merchant in Haddington, East Lothian, sederunt book, 1810-1811. [NRS.CS6.688]

CARPHIN, JOHN, a Second Lieutenant of the Royal Linlithgow Volunteers, was admitted as a burgess and guilds-brother of Dunfermline, Fife, on 15 August 1804. [DM]

CARRICK, FRANCIS, a smith in Dunbar, East Lothian, was accused of rioting in Dunbar in 1816. [NRS.SC40.54.1.32]

CARRUTHERS, MARGARET, daughter of Reverend William Carruthers in South Queensferry, West Lothian, wife of Capitao Tenente Jose Maria de Conceicao, died in Rio de Janeiro, Brazil, on 11 October 1877. [S.10710]

CARSS, GEORGE, in Dunbar, East Lothian, was accused of rioting in Dunbar in 1816. [NRS.SC40.54.1.32]

CARTER, WALTER, born 19 May 1823 in Earlston, Berwickshire, son of Thomas Carter and his wife Agnes Ewing, emigrated to America in 1831, settled in Saratoga County, New York, did at Montclair, New Jersey, on 19 May 1823. [ANY]

CHAPMAN, DAVID, born 1817, from Bathgate, West Lothian, later in Hopetoun Sawmills, Port Esperance, died in Hobart, Tasmania, Australia, on 24 June 1884. [S.12823]

CHAPMAN, THOMAS, born in 1836, a merchant in Monte Video, Uruguay, died in Barnton, West Lothian, on 19 January 1874, testament, 1874, Edinburgh, [NRS.SC70.1.1879.102]

CHAPMAN, WILLIAM, [1847-1916], and his wife Annie Johnston, [1842-1920], in Grangemouth, West Lothian. [Polmont gravestone]

CHARLES, DUNCAN, a baker in Musselburgh, Mid Lothian, father of Duncan Charles a baker in Alexandria, Virginia, in 1802, also in 1808 [NRS.CS17.1.21/268; 27/252]

CHARLES, GEORGE, a butcher in Musselburgh, Mid Lothian, by 1797, previously in Alexandria, Fairfax County, Virginia. [NRS.CS17.1.16/213]

CHARLES, JAMES, a baker in Charleston, South Carolina, appointed William Charles and John Charles, butchers in Musselburgh, Mid Lothian, as his attorney on 28 March 1793. [NRS.RD4.254.393]

CHARTERS, JAMES, schoolmaster in Esply, Northumberland, brother and heir of John Charters, a servant in Thirlstane, sons of John Charters, a herd at Yetholm, Roxburghshire, 27 March 1790. [NRS.S/H]

CHARTERS, MARY JANE, only daughter of Thomas Charters a merchant in Roxburghshire, married Alexander Jardine a merchant in St John, New Brunswick, there on 19 August 1845. [W.609]

CHARTERIS, JANE, eldest daughter of Thomas Charteris, a merchant in Berwick, was married there on 15 October 1822 to Thomas Hunter, a merchant in Glasgow. [SM.90.631]

CHRISTIE, JOHN, a farmer in Primrose, Carrington, Mid Lothian, applied to settle in Canada on 9 March 1815. [NRS.RH9]

CHRISTIE, RICHARD, born 1796, a joiner, died on 20 September 1852. Husband of Jane Henderson, born 1797, died 8 January 1823. [Garvald gravestone, East Lothian]

CHRISTIE, T., second son of John Christie at Hailes Quarry, Mid Lothian, a surgeon in Hanover Town, Virginia, died on 3 February 1812. [SM.74.479]

CHRISTISON, ALEXANDER, born 17 April 1826 in Foulden, Berwickshire, son of Reverend Alexander Christison and his wife Helen Cameron, died in Australia. [F.2.49]

CHRISTISON, CAMERON, born 30 January 1839 in Foulden, Berwickshire, son of Reverend Alexander Christison and his wife Helen Cameron, was killed in China by pirates on 15 November 1860. [F.2.49] [Foulden gravestone]

CHRISTISON, ROBERT, born 8 January 1837, son of Reverend Alexander Christison and his wife Helen Cameron, an explorer and pastoral pioneer of

North West Queensland, Australia, died 25 October 1915. [Foulden gravestone, Berwickshire]

CHRISTISON, THOMAS MCKNIGHT, born 15 April 1835 in Foulden, Berwickshire, son of Reverend Alexander Christison and his wife Helen Cameron, a sheep farmer who died in Australia in 1886. [F.2.49]

CHRISTISON, WILLIAM CAMERON, born 18 June 1827 in Foulden, Berwickshire, son of Reverend Alexander Christison and his wife Helen Cameron, was drowned crossing the River Burdekin, Queensland, Australia, on 3 February 1874. [F.2.49] [Foulden gravestone]

CLAPERTON, ALEXANDER, a storekeeper in Empire City, Kansas, son and heir of Thomas Claperton, a cooper in Gorebridge, Mid Lothian, who died on 19 August 1875. [NRS.S/H]

CLAPPERTON, DAVID, born 1746, a mason, died in March 1812, husband of Christian Skead, born 1741, died on 2 February 1800. [Innerwick gravestone, East Lothian]

CLARK, GEORGE, a butcher in Detroit, Michigan, nephew and heir of William Murray, a smith in Fisherrow, Mid Lothian, who died on 30 October 1851. [NRS.S/H]

CLARKE, GEORGE M., born 1829, from Musselburgh, Mid Lothian, and Portobello, Mid Lothian, died in Detroit, Michigan, on 11 February 1885. [S.13000]

CLARK, JOHN, in Eyemouth, Berwickshire, papers, 1839. [NRS.GD267.24.2]

CLARK, WILLIAM, a Captain of the Royal Navy, married Jane Tod, a spinster in Dunbar, East Lothian, there on 19 May 1790, witnesses were Thomas Tod and Alexander Tod. [NRS.CH12.2.2.18] [HEC]

CLARK, WILLIAM, with his wife and three children, from Berwick-on-Tweed, Northumberland, emigrated via Greenock aboard the Portaferry to Quebec in May 1832. [QM.13.6.1832]

CLARKSON, JAMES, born 1835, an assistant surgeon aboard HMS Orpheus who was drowned off New Zealand on 2 February 1863. [Selkirk gravestone]

CLAZY, GEORGE, born 1764, died 3 October 1833, husband of Agnes Alexander, born 1769, died 1 October 1852. [Eccles gravestone, Berwickshire]

CLEGHORN, DAVID, born 1794 in Haddington, East Lothian, a publican in Front Street there, was accused of mobbing and rioting there in 1831. [NRS.AD14.3358]

CLEGHORN, JAMES, from Pentland Denhead, later in St Phillipe, Montreal, Quebec, died in New Glasgow, Montreal, on 26 May 1849. [SG.18.1838]

CLEGHORN, JOHN, son of John Cleghorn a farmer in Corstorphine, Mid Lothian, was apprenticed to Robert Cleghorn, a baker in Edinburgh, for five years, on 13 May 1790. [ERA]

CLERK of Penicuik muniments, Mid Lothian, [NRS.GD18]

CLUNIE, ROBERT DUNDAS, in the West Indies, youngest son of Reverend John Clunie in Borthwick, Mid Lothian, appointed his brother James Oliphant Clunie in Edinburgh, as his attorney, subscribed in Millwards Bog Estate, St Dorothy's, Jamaica, on 22 October 1819. [NRS.RD5.175.73]

CLYDESDALE, or MITCHELL, C., in New York, heir to her father H. Clydesdale, a former sailor of the Royal Navy, in Penicuik, Mid Lothian, in 1847. [NRS.S/H]

COCHRAN, ALEXANDER, born 18 August 1790, son of Reverend John Cochran and his wife Catherine Miller in Oldhamstocks, East Lothian, a merchant who died in the Canary Islands. [F.1.413]

COCHRANE, DAVID, in Virginia, heir of Henry Cochrane of Barbauchlaw, East Lothian, 1784, 1789, 1790. [NRS.CS17,1.3/314; CS17.1.359; CS17.1.9.82]

COCHRANE, JAMES, probably from Tranent, East Lothian, a planter in North Carolina before 1798, probate 29 March 1798, South Carolina.

COCHRANE, GEORGE, son of George Cochrane a vintner in Musselburgh, Mid Lothian, was apprenticed to James Cowan, a candlemaker in Edinburgh, for five years, on 6 June 1793. [ERA]

COCHRANE, RICHARD, formerly a Judge of the Court of Common Pleas in New Jersey, died in Dalkeith, Mid Lothian, in October 1804. [AJ.2962]

COCKBURN, Dr ALEXANDER, born in August 1739 in Duns, Berwickshire, son of William Cockburn and his wife Barbara Home, married Elizabeth Kennedy, daughter of Thomas Kennedy of Maybole, Ayrshire, in Edinburgh on 7 November 1773, possibly emigrated via Plymouth aboard the Lawrent to Grenada, on 9 January 1774, [TNA.T47.9/11]; died in St George, Grenada on 8 November 1815. [CFR] [AJ.3551] [EMR]

COCKBURN, HENRY, born 1801 in Haddington, East Lothian, was educated at Edinburgh University, minister of St Andrew's, Grenada from 1838 until his death on 19 July 1854. [F.7.667]

COCKBURN, JOHN, a shepherd from Mellerstain, Roxburghshire, with Jane his wife, and seven children, emigrated via Greenock to Canada in 1815. [TNA.CO385.2]

COCKBURN, LAWRENCE, born 1822, fifth son of Lord Cockburn, died in Brighton, Melbourne, Victoria, Australia, on 2 September 1871. [AJ.6461]

COCKBURN, ROBERT, born 1778, schoolmaster in Garvald for 45 years, died on 16 May 1845. [Garvald gravestone, East Lothian]

COCKFIELD, THOMAS NELSON, born 1822, eldest son of Edward Cockfield in Dunbar, East Lothian, a merchant in St Kitts, died there on 27 October 1853. [EEC.22514]; testament, 1869, Edinburgh. [NRS.SC70.1.142/861]

COLIN, THOMAS, a fisherman in Eyemouth, Berwickshire, testament, 1808, Comm. Lauder. [NRS]

CONDIE, WILLIAM, born 1792, a joiner in Portobello, Mid Lothian, died 10 December 1845. [Duddingston gravestone]

COOK, GEORGE FREDERICK, born 1755 in Berwick on Tweed, Northumberland, a tragedian, died in New York on 26 September 1812. [GM.82.494]

COOPER, MARGARET, daughter of Arthur Cooper in St Croix, Danish West Indies, married Dr Charles Kennedy, a physician in St Croix, in Eyemouth, Berwickshire, in October 1797. [EEC.392]

CORBETT, WILLIAM, in Melville Street, Portobello, Mid Lothian, father of George Corbett, who married Helen Margaret McGregor, fourth daughter of J. W. McGregor in Glasgow, in Buenos Ayres, Argentina, on 8 June 1871. [S.8725]; parents of five children born at the Estancia de los Inglesias, Buenos Ayres between 1872 and 1883. [S]

COSSAR, HELLEN, born 1840, daughter of David Cossar, [1810-1906], a feuar in Coldingham, Berwickshire, and his wife Ann Law, [1811-1849], died in Memphis, Tennessee, on 20 September 1878. [Coldingham gravestone]

COSSAR, ROBERT, a merchant in Greenlaw, Berwickshire, testament, 1791, Comm. Lauder. [NRS]

COWAN, ALEXANDER, born 1793, son of Thomas Cowan the Customs Controller in Bo'ness, West Lothian, [1757-1828], and his wife Agnes Drummond, [1762-1799], died in St John's, New Brunswick, on 29 June 1810. [Bo'ness gravestone]

COWAN, CHARLES, born 1806, son of Thomas Cowan the Customs Controller in Bo'ness, [1757-1828], and his wife Agnes Drummond, [1762-1799], died in Sierra Leone, in December 1828. [Bo'ness gravestone, West Lothian]

COWAN, JAMES, the younger, son of Thomas Cowan a butcher in Musselburgh, Mid Lothian, was apprenticed to James Cowan, a candlemaker in Edinburgh, for five years, on 11 July 1799. [ERA]

COWAN, JOHN, born 1783 in Grangemouth, Bo'ness, West Lothian, a seaman was accused of theft from the schooner Active of Belfast in 1830. [NRS.AD14.30.141]

COWAN, THOMAS, the Customs Controller in Bo'ness, West Lothian, father of Charles Cowan, born 1806, died in December 1828 in Sierra Leone. [Bo'ness gravestone, West Lothian]

COWAN, THOMAS, Captain of the Royal Linlithgow Volunteers, was admitted as a burgess and guilds-brother of Dunfermline, Fife, on 15 August 1804. [DM]

COWAN, WILLIAM, son of Thomas Cowan a butcher in Musselburgh, Mid Lothian, was apprenticed to Alexander Douglas, a candlemaker in Edinburgh, for six years, on 26 June 1794. [ERA]

26

COWIE, THOMAS, a cabinetmaker, in Hamilton, Canada West, son and heir of Walkinshaw Cowie, a spirit dealer in Corstorphine, Mid Lothian, who died in 1843. [NRS.S/H]

CRAIG, DAVID, in New Providence, Bahamas, grandson and heir of David Craig, a gardener in Pilrig, Mid Lothian, in 1802. [NRS.S/H]

CRAIG, JOHN MOORE, son of John Craig in Prestonholm, died at the Cape of Good Hope, South Africa, on 10 February 1845. [EEC.21178]

CRANSTOUN, GEORGE, youngest son of Reverend Cranstoun in Ancrum, Roxburghshire, died on Great Exuma Island in the Bahamas, on 10 April 1790. [SM.52.412]

CRAW, JAMES, at the Cape of Good Hope, South Africa, son of Reverend Peter Craw in St Boswell's, Roxburghshire, who died on 21 March 1834. [NRS.S/H]

CRAW, JOHN, MD, born 1842, son of John Craw of Lanton Tower, of the Royal Navy, died in Malta on 1 July 1874. [Greenlaw gravestone, Berwickshire]

CRAWFORD, ALEXANDER, in North Berwick, East Lothian, sequestration in 1820. [NRS.CS236.C.2210]

CRAWFORD, ELIZABETH, second daughter of William Crawford in Glasgow, married George C. Thorburn from New York, in Earlston, Berwickshire, on 16 July 1819. [S.132.19]

CRAWFORD, HUGH, son of William Crawford in Chicago, Illinois, cousin and heir of William Shaw, only child of George Shaw, a sailor in Bo'ness, West Lothian, in 1867. [NRS.S/H]

CREAK, WILLIAM, born 1838, son of Thomas Creak of Whitrig, [1774-1849], was drowned in the Burry River in the Cape of Good Hope, South Africa, on 16 June 1864. [Eccles gravestone, Berwickshire]

CRICHTON, DAVID, son of David Crichton, a merchant in Dalkeith, Mid Lothian, died in Demerara on 25 October 1802. [EA.4074.03]

CRICHTON, JOHN, born 1801, son of John Crichton, [1765-1826], and his wife Margaret Purves, [1777-1807], died in Brockville, Canada West, on 16 April 1854. [Chirnside gravestone, Berwickshire]

CROOKS, JAMES. born 1822, son of James Crooks, [1788-1854], a merchant in Cockburnspath, and his wife Agnes Crerar, [1785-1847], died in Collingwood, New Zealand, on 12 March 1861. [Cockburnspath gravestone, Berwickshire]

CROOKS, JANE, born 1810, daughter of James Crooks, [1788-1854], a merchant in Cockburnspath, and his wife Agnes Crerar, [1785-1847], died in St Louis, Missouri, on 26 June 1849. [Cockburnspath gravestone, Berwickshire]

CROSBIE, JAMES, son of Reverend John Crosbie [1806-1872], was drowned in Vackadandah Creek, New South Wales, Australia, in September 1863. [Garvald gravestone, East Lothian]

CROSSLEY, JOHN, a butcher and vintner in Cramond, West Lothian, a decreet in 1833. [NRS.CS46.1833.3.29]

CRUICKSHANK, GEORGE, son of James Cruickshank the parochial schoolmaster of Mid Calder, West Lothian, died in Spanish Town, Jamaica, on 11 April 1823. [S.346.288]

CUMING, ALEXANDER, First Lieutenant of the Royal Linlithgow Volunteers, was admitted as a burgess and guilds-brother of Dunfermline, Fife, on 15 August 1804. [DM]

CUMMING, ROBERT, a Lieutenant of the Royal Navy, residing in Musselburgh, Mid Lothian, versus Ann Reid, daughter of James Reid a coachmaker in Canongate, Edinburgh, deceased, a process of separation and aliment, 2 March 1789. [NRS.CC8.6.829]

CUNNINGHAM, ARCHIBALD, born 1795, emigrated from Linlithgow, West Lothian, to America in 1818. [BAF]

CUNNINGHAM, GEORGE, born 14 November 1804 in Duns, Berwickshire, son of Reverend George Cunningham and his wife Hyndmer Barclay, died in Canada. [F.2.11]

CUNNINGHAM, JAMES, grandson of Margaret Cleghorn, [1723-1803], settled in Jamaica before 1803. [Kirkliston gravestone, West Lothian]

CUNNINGHAM, JAMES, born 1802, a bank agent and surveyor in Coldstream, Berwickshire, died 23 January 1876, husband of Agnes Small, born 1798, died 30 May 1829. [Eccles gravestone, Berwickshire]

CUNNINGHAM, JANE, daughter of John Cunningham in Dirleton, East Lothian, married John Bruce from St Elizabeth, Jamaica, in Dirleton on 12 January 1817. [S.51.18]

CUNNINGHAM, JOHN, born in Currie, Mid Lothian, died at Montego Bay, St James, Jamaica, on 8 December 1790. [Montego Bay gravestone]

CUNNINGHAM, JOHN, born 1738 in Kirknewton, Mid Lothian, died in 1812. [Montego Bay gravestone, Jamaica]

CUPPLES, Reverend JOHN, minister at Swinton, Berwickshire, testament, 1799, Comm. Lauder. [NRS]

CURLE, J., agent for the British Linen Company in Melrose, Roxburghshire, in 1849. [POD]

CURRIE, GEORGE, second son of William Currie in Greenland, Roxburghshire, died in New Orleans, Louisiana, in January 1829. [EEC.18655]

CURRIE, GEORGE, born 1 January 1823 in Howford, died in Australia on 10 April 1908, buried at Denilquin, New South Wales, Australia. [Selkirk gravestone]

CUSHNY, THOMAS, born 31 March 1812, son of Arthur Cushny and his wife Alison Minto, died in Natchez, Mississippi, in October 1837. [Peebles gravestone]

CUTHBERTSON, GEORGE DOUGLAS, born 1851 son of James Cuthbertson, a medical student from Inveresk, Musselburgh, Mid Lothian, died on Estancia de los Menrios, Pysander, Uruguay, on 24 January 1871. [S.8636]

CUTHILL, WILLIAM, a secretary in Dalkeith, Mid Lothian, letters, 1811-1828. [NRS.GD224.662]

DALL, JAMES, agent for the Western Bank of Scotland in North Berwick, East Lothian, in 1849. [POD]

DALRYMPLE, Sir HEW HAMILTON, of Bargany and North Berwick, East Lothian, probate, 22 April 1800. [NRS.GD2.67]

DALRYMPLE, JOHN HAMILTON, the Collector of Customs, son of Hew Dalrymple of Nunraw, died at Montego Bay, Jamaica, on 7 August 1804. [SM.66.885]

DALRYMPLE, Sir JOHN, of North Berwick, husband of Charlotte Warrender, a letter dated 1834. [NRS.GD110.1137]

DARLING, ANDREW, died on the island of St Helena on 12 August 1841. [Kelso gravestone, Roxburghshire]

DARLING, ROBERT, born 1797, son of Thomas Darling and his wife Isobel Ponton, died in Jamaica on 2 August 1821. [Chirnside gravestone, Berwickshire]

DARLING, Professor WILLIAM, MD, FRCS, born 1804 in Duns, Berwickshire, died at the University of New York on 25 December 1884. [S.12958]

DAVIDSON, ALEXANDER, born 21 January 1849 in Abbey St Bathans, Berwickshire, son of Reverend Thomas Davidson and his wife Henrietta Proudfoot, a banker in South Africa. [F.2.3]

DAVIDSON, BENJAMIN, a carter in Pot Close, Sprouston, Roxburghshire, was accused of reckless driving between Jedfoot Bridge and Crailing, in 1829. [NRS.AD14.29.216]

DAVIDSON, JOHN, a merchant in Eyemouth, Berwickshire, testament, 1798, Comm. Lauder. [NRS]

DAVIDSON, MICHAEL, born 1821, died in Nether Horsburgh on 13 December 1869, husband of Ann Tait who died in New Zealand aged 72. [Innerleithen gravestone, Peebles-shire]

DAVIDSON, THOMAS, born 1801, died in Bemes, Massachusetts, on 9 August 1889. [Ancrum gravestone, Roxburghshire]

DAVIDSON, WILLIAM, the younger, son and heir of John Davidson of Halltree, a Writer to the Signet, heir to lands in the lordship of Jedburgh, Roxburghshire, 4 October 1792. [NRS.S/H]

DAVIDSON, WILLIAM, a farmer at Caversbarre, son and heir of William Davidson a vintner in Melrose, Roxburghshire, 1846. [NRS.S/H]

DAVIDSON, WILLIAM PROUDFOOT, born 18 September 1853 in Abbey St Bathans, Berwickshire, son of Reverend Thomas Davidson and his wife Henrietta Proudfoot, died in Queensland, Australia. [F.2.3]

DAWSON, ELIZABETH, relict of Robert French late of Tortula, testament, 1821, Comm. Lauder. [NRS]

DEAN, JAMES ALEXANDER, son of John Dean, a railway contractor in Linlithgow, West Lothian, was educated at Marischal College, Aberdeen, in 1859, settled in South Africa. [MCA]

DEANS, HENRY, [1826-1872], and his wife Mary Martin Dudgeon, [1830-1900], parents of Henry Cecil Deans, born 1864, died in Spokane, Washington, on 12 November 1891. [Dirleton gravestone, East Lothian]

DEANS, JAMES, a painter in Haddington, East Lothian, a summons for payment due against Captain William Frederick Brown in North Berwick, East Lothian, in 1834. [NRS.AD14.34.24]

DENHAM, ANDREW, jr., a wood merchant and wholesale spirit dealer in Dunbar, East Lothian, sederunt books, 1835-1837.[NRS.CS96.4197]

DENHAM, JANE, daughter of Andrew Denham in Dunbar, East Lothian, wife of Dr Palmer, died in Monticello, Florida, on 20 August 1860. [W.XXI.2232]

DENHOLM, GRACE, eldest daughter of H. Denholm of Birthwood, married Robert Paterson a merchant in Quebec, at Birthwood on 11 March 1822. [S.271.102]

DICK, AGNES HENDERSON, born 1838, daughter of William Dick and his wife Jane S. Brash in Dryburgh Mains, wife of S. J. Wills, died in Queensland, Australia, on 28 September 1869. [Uphall gravestone, West Lothian]

DICK, JAMES, born 1777, son of John Dick in Bathgate, West Lothian, emigrated with his wife and family to Canada in 1821, settled in Prescott, was drowned in June 1821 at Lachine, buried in Lanark, Ontario. [SG]

DICK, JOHN, born 1803, son of John Dick in Bathgate, West Lothian, emigrated to Canada in 1821, husband of Mary Gemmell, [1809-1853], died in Lanark, Ontario, in 1862. [SG]

DICK, RICHARD, son of George Dick a shoemaker in Jedburgh, Roxburghshire, later a carpenter in America in 1807. [NRS.CS17.1.26/355]

DICK, WILLIAM, born 1779, son of John Dick, [1747-1833], and his wife Janet Dick, [1742-1828], in Bathgate, West Lothian, died in Jamaica in 1803. [Bathgate, Kirkton, gravestone]

DICKSON, ALEXANDER, born 1781, son of Peter Dickson, a farmer, and his wife Ann Dewar, formerly an engineer in Berlin, Germany, died in Wheatlands, Kirkliston, West Lothian, on 6 January 1824. [Kirkliston gravestone]

DICKSON, Reverend JOHN, born 1779, a missionary for 24 years to the Moslems in South Russia, he translated the Bible into Tartar Turkish, died in Edinburgh on 31 January 1838. [Eddleston gravestone, Peebles-shire]

DICKSON, RALPH, a weaver in Sprouston, Roxburghshire, brother and heir of John Dickson a weaver there, 1843. [NRS.S/H]

DICKSON, ROBERT, a tailor and publican in Penicuik, Mid Lothian, versus his wife Jean Glenny, a Process of Separation in 1820. [NRS.CC8.6.1782]

DINNET, ROBERT, a carrier in Dunbar, East Lothian, was accused of the murder of Francis Findlay in Dunbar, East Lothian, in 1824. [NRS.AD14.24.372]

DIXON, JOHN, in Kingston, North Berwick, East Lothian, a letter, 1835. [NRS.GD152.53.2.6]

DOBSON, FRANCIS, and Euphemia Turnbull, both from Selkirk, Selkirkshire, were married in Halifax, Nova Scotia, on 17 June 1818. [AR.27.6.1818]

DODDS, CATHERINE, born 1839, from Berwickshire, died in Buenos Ayres, Argentina, in 1871. [SRP.365]

DODS, JAMES, son of Peter Dods in Haddington, East Lothian died in Berea, Ohio, on 6 August 1849. [DGH.13.9.1849]

DODDS, JOHN, blacksmith in Galashiels, Selkirkshire, son and heir of James Dodds a spinner in Jedburgh, Roxburghshire, 1840. [NRS.S/H]

DODS, Dr ROBERT, from Prora, East Lothian, died in New Windsor, Maryland, on 27 July 1833. [AJ.4471]

DODS, WILLIAM, in Haddington, East Lothian, a victim of rioting and mobbing there in 1831. [NRS.AD14.3.358]

DODS, Miss, youngest daughter of Mr Dods of Seton Hill, East Lothian, died at Cote de la Visitation, Montreal, on 5 March 1855. [EEC.22715]

DONALDSON, GEORGE, son of Alexander Donaldson and his wife Agnes Wightman, [1731-1809], in Coldstream, Berwickshire, settled in Jamaica. [Lennell gravestone, Berwickshire]

DONALDSON, ROBERT, born 1826, died in Otago, New Zealand, on 16 June 1862. [Ettrick gravestone, Selkirkshire]

DOUGLAS, ADAM, youngest son of Adam T. Douglas in Moneylaws, died in Buenos Ayres, Argentina, on 13 April 1871. [S.8677]

DOUGLAS, CHARLES, born 1799, a mug-selling tinker in Jedburgh, Dumfries-shire, was accused of rioting and assault at Jedburgh Tollhouse in 1829. [NRS.AD14.29.210]

DOUGLAS, DAVID, a mug selling tinker in Kirk Yetholm, Dumfries-shire, was accused of rioting and assault at Jedburgh Tollhouse in 1829. [NRS.AD14.29.210]

DOUGLAS, DONALD, a labourer in Broxburn, West Lothian, was accused of assault a petition in 1823. [NRS.B48.16.6.4]

DOUGLAS, GEORGE BRUCE, son of William Bruce in Portobello, Mid Lothian, married Henrietta Louisa Scott, daughter of William Scott in New York, there on 2 December 1858. [W.XIX.2043]

DOUGLAS, Mrs HELEN, spouse to James Baillie of Olivebank, versus Mrs Elizabeth Chalmers, widow of Archibald Scott a surgeon in Musselburgh, Mid Lothian, 16 July 1789. [NRS.CC8.6.789]

DOUGLAS, JAMES, born 1776 in the Lothians, a turner who was naturalised in Charleston, South Carolina, on 16 October 1805. [NARA.M1183.1]

DOUGLAS, JAMES, formerly a Major in the Service of the East India Company in Bombay, later in Edenside, Kelso, Roxburghshire, died in May 1814, sederunt book. [NRS.GD282.12.132]

DOUGLAS, JAMES, from Kirkcudbright, was educated at Theological Hall from 1808 to 1812, ordained in 1813, a minister in Chirnside, Roxburghshire, emigrated to America in 1818. [UPC]

DOUGLAS, JAMES, agent for the Commercial Bank of Scotland, in Kelso, Roxburghshire, in 1849. [POD]

DOUGLAS, JOHN, a labourer in Broxburn, West Lothian, was accused of assault a petition in 1823. [NRS.B48.16.6.4]

DOUGLAS, ROBERT, in Berwick-on-Tweed, Northumberland, a former soldier of the 68th Regiment, with his wife and two children, applied to settle in Canada on 3 October 1827. [TNA.CO384.5.807]

DOUGLAS, THOMASINA, wife of David Douglas a mug-selling tinker, in Kirk Yetholm, Dumfries-shire, was accused of rioting and assault at Jedburgh Tollhouse, Roxburghshire, in 1829. [NRS.AD14.29.210]

DOWNIE, ALEXANDER, a shoemaker in Linlithgow, West Lothian, was accused of stealing beef in 1825. [NRS.B48.16.6.6]

DRUMMOND, ROBERT, in Grangepans, West Lothian, dead by 1807 father of John Drummond in Brunswick, Virginia. [NRS.S/H]

DRYSDALE, ANDREW, formerly a farmer in Middleton, Mid Lothian, died in Beaufort, South Carolina, in 1821. [BM.40.264] [EEC.17259]

DRYSDALE, HELEN, born 16 February 1783, in Howlams, Berwickshire, died in Leith on 1 February 1819, wife of George Carstairs. [South Leith gravestone]

DRYSDALE, JOHN, born 2 July 1833, died IN Buenos Ayres, Argentina, on 22 March 1893. [Preston Kirk gravestone, East Lothian]

DRYDEN, ROBERT, born 11 January 1784 in St Boswells, Roxburghshire, son of Thomas Dryden and his wife Jean Thomson, married Alison Young in 1814, emigrated to Canada in 1818. [SG]

DUDGEON, FRANCIS ALEXANDER, born 1833m died in Sydney, New South Wales, Australia, on 21 December 1855. [Kelso gravestone, Roxburghshire]

DUDGEON, GEORGE and ROBERT, in Swineburn, Kirkliston, West Lothian, wee victim of poachers in 1830. [NRS.AD14.30.260]

DUDGEON, JOHN, a Writer to the Signet, married Isabella Falconer, daughter of John Falconer a merchant in Glasgow, in Cherrytrees, Roxburghshire, on 22 October 1822. [SM.90.631]

DUDGEON, WILLIAM, a shepherd at Garvald Grange, East Lothian, versus Mary Sives in Whittinghame, East Lothian, a Process of Divorce in 1804. [NRS.CC8.6.1196]

DUNBAR, Captain DUNBAR, son of the Earl of Selkirk, died in St Kitts in November 1796. [GM.67.80]

DUNBAR, JAMES, was granted a lease of Middle Pocklaw, Eyemouth, Berwickshire, in 1847. [NRS.267.27.241.38.26]

DUNCAN, Reverend ADAM, in Kirkliston, West Lothian, a letter dated 1830. [NRS.GD1.582/3]

DUNCAN, GEORGE, a labourer in South Queensferry, West Lothian, was accused of poaching at Bittermillfield, Dalmeny, West Lothian, in 1841. [NRS.AD14.41.120]

DUNCAN, THOMAS, late in Grenada, died in Leathcote, West Lothian, on 17 June 1849. [SG.1831]; Letters from Thomas Duncan in Grenada to George Home of Branxton from 1804 to 1818. [NRS.GD267.5.12]

DUNCAN, WILLIAM, born 31 December 1747, son of Reverend Alexander Duncan and his wife Helen Home in Smailholm, Roxburghshire, a Colonel in East India Company Service, died in London on 1 March 1830. [F.2.162]

DUNCAN, WILLIAM, born 1831, younger son of Peter Duncan in Westfield, Linlithgow, West Lothian, died in La Noria, Iquiqie, Peru, on 27 January 1879. [S.11129]

DUNDAS, JAMES, of Dundas, was admitted as a burgess of Linlithgow, West Lothian, in 1826. [NRS.GD75.399]

DUNDAS, JOHN, son of Patrick Dundas a surgeon in Linlithgow, West Lothian, in the Service of the East India Company in Bencoola, Sumatra, testament, 1788, Comm. Edinburgh. [NRS]

DUNLOP, THOMAS, son of John Dunlop a farmer in Chisholm, Roxburghshire, was apprenticed to George Dunlop a merchant in Edinburgh for five years on 15 August 1799. [ERA]

DUNLOP, WILLIAM, born 1775, fourth son of David Dunlop, [1739-1804], a farmer in Loans, and his wife Agnes Dickie, [1752-1798], died on Grenada in 1790. [Dundonald gravestone, Ayrshire]

DUNLOP, Colonel WILLIAM, born 16 March 1785 in Whitmuirhall, Selkirkshire, Quartermaster General of the Bengal Army in the Service of the East India Company, died in Allahabad, India, on 5 November 1841. [St Andrews Kirk gravestone, Calcutta.]

EASTON, ANDREW, born 1813, farm steward at Eccles Tofts, died on 11 May 1871, husband of Alison Proudfoot, born 1812, died at Greenlaw on 30 September 1882. [Eccles gravestone, Berwickshire]

EASTON, THOMAS, a painter in Dunbar, East Lothian, father of William Easton, a merchant who died in Monte Video, Uruguay, on 12 August 1879. [S.11296]

ECKURN, JAMES, born 1800 in Roxburghshire, emigrated aboard the Brilliant to East Cape Colony, South Africa, in 1820, settled on the Baviaans River. [ScotGen.30.1.32]

EDGAR, JOHN, a surgeon in Ayr, married Anna Dunlop, daughter of John Dunlop in St Croix, Danish West Indies, in Irvine, Ayrshire, on 9 November 1821. [AJ.3854] [S.253.374]

EDINGTON, PETER, in North Berwick, East Lothian, a victim of forgery in 1840. [NRS.AD14.40.319]

ELDER, JAMES, born 1824, a farm labourer from Peebles, landed in Hobart, Tasmania, Australia, from the White Star on 28 July 1855. [SRA.TD292]

ELDER, JAMES, born on 13 January 1782 in West Linton, Peebles-shire, son of William Elder and his wife Elizabeth Thomson, emigrated to America in 1815, a tanner in Charleston, South Carolina, was naturalised on 6 October 1830, died on 12 March 1850. [NARA.M1183.1] [Second Presbyterian gravestone, Charleston]

ELLIOT, AGNES, at Marchcleugh, Roxburghshire, widow of John Bell in Lanton Park, daughter of John Elliot and his wife Marion Herbertson, sister and heir of Margaret Elliot, 1841. [NRS.S/H]

ELLIOT, CHARLOTTE, daughter of Adam Elliot a merchant in Danzig brother of Robert Elliot a merchant in Amsterdam, Holland, lately of Pinnaclehill, Roxburghshire, heir to her uncle the said Robert Elliot who died 30 October 1823. [NRS.S/H]

ELLIOT, JAMES, born 1789 in Portobello, Mid Lothian, a Lieutenant Colonel of the Trelawney Militia in Jamaica, died on 2 June 1862, husband of Margaret Hunter, born 1797, died 1885. [Portobello Episcopal gravestone]

ELLIOT, JANE ANNE, born 14 December 1816, in Genoa, Italy, daughter of George Elliot and his wife Eliza, died at Minto, Roxburghshire, on 18 January 1820. [Kelso Episcopal gravestone]

ELLIOT, JOHN, born 1803, from Kelso, Roxburghshire, died in Tuscumba, Alabama, on 21 September 1839. [EEC.19976]

ELLIOT, MARY, daughter of Ralph Elliot, deceased, a shipmaster in Musselburgh, Mid Lothian, versus Peter Taylor a wright in Leith, Midlothian, who married on 11 January 1793, a process of divorce, 1 and 29 April 1796. [NRS.CC8.6.976]

ELLIOT, ROBERT, born 1809, son of Robert Elliot of Hermitage, [1760-1824], and his wife Mary Scott, [1786-1843], died in Madeira on 28 January 1844. [Kelso gravestone, Roxburghshire]

ELLIOTT, Sir WILLIAM, heir to his father Sir Francis Elliott of Stobs, Roxburghshire, 11 August 1791. [NRS.S/H]

EMOND, ROBERT, born 1795 in Selkirk, a grocer and draper in North Berwick, East Lothian, was accuse of the murder of his sister-in-law Katherine Franks, and her daughter Magdelina, in the Abbey of Haddington in 1830. [NRS.AD14.30.23]

ERSKINE, J., agent for the British Linen Company in Melrose, Selkirkshire, in 1849. [POD]

EWART, DAVID, born 1810, son of George Ewart, [1779-1844], a saddler and ironmonger in Duns, Berwickshire, and his wife Catherine Hogg, [1788-1824], died in Antigua on 2 August 1835. [Duns gravestone, Berwickshire]

EWART, JOHN, son of Isabella Lanford or Ewart in Berwick-on-Tweed, Northumberland, settled in Albany, New York, probate May 1825, PCC. [TNA]

FAIRBAIRN, ANDREW, son of William Fairbairn a schoolmaster in Galashiels, Selkirkshire, was apprenticed to John Turnbull, a merchant in Edinburgh, for five years on 12 December 1799. [ERA]

FAIRBAIRN, ANDREW, born 1814, died on 15 April 1899, husband of Jane Douglas, born 1793, died on 18 February 1857. [Eccles gravestone, Berwickshire]

FAIRBAIRN, JOHN, son of Reverend John Fairbairn in Greenlaw, Berwickshire, was educated at Marischal College, Aberdeen, in 1854, later a merchant in Rockhampton, Queensland, Australia, died on 1 January 1901. [F.2.21] [MCA]

FAIRHOLME, GEORGE K. E., third son of George Fairholme of Greenknowe, Berwickshire, married Pauline Anelia Poellnitz, eldest daughter of Baron Frederic Poellnitz of Chateau Frankenberg, Bavaria, at the British Embassy, Frankfurt, Germany, on 14 January 1857. [W.XVIII.1834]; later, of Old Melrose, Roxburghshire, father of a daughter born in Wurzburg, Bavaria, on 23 May 1861. [Hawick Advertiser, Roxburghshire] [W.XXII.2309]; also, father of a son born in Wurzburg in 1862. [Hawick Advertiser]

FAIRNINGTON, JOHN, a horse thief, was sentenced at Jedburgh, Roxburghshire, to transportation to the colonies for 14 years, in October 1790. [AJ.2230]

FALCONER, RICHARD, a publican in Linlithgow, West Lothian, was summoned at the instance of his creditors William Glen and Company, distillers in Mains, in 1815. [NRS.GD215.231]

FALL, JOHN, born 1777 in Roxburghshire, a carpenter who emigrated via London to America, was naturalised in New York on 16 June 1825. [NARA]

FERGUSON, ANGUS, son of Reverend John Ferguson in Uphall, West Lothian, died in Jamaica on 28 June 1819. [S.3.143]

FERGUSON, DAVID, a civil engineer, third son of James Ferguson in Bathgate, West Lothian, died at Point St Charles, Montreal, Quebec, on 5 April 1859. [CM.21712]

FERGUSON, ROBERT, second son of Thomas Ferguson in Young Street, Peebles, formerly of Leith, late of Manchester, Jamaica, died in Howard House, Detroit, Michigan, on 12 September 1855. [EEC.322800]

FERME, MARY, fourth daughter of George Ferme in Braidwood, married Henry P. Palmer from Grenada, in Braidwood on 14 December 1818. [DPCA.870]

FIFE, JAMES, from Haddington, East Lothian, died in Charleston, South Carolina, on 18 December 1804. [SM.67.565] [Old Scots gravestone, Charleston] [AJ.2992]

FINLAY, ANN, from Wallyford, East Lothian, died on Madeira on 12 April 1810. [ARM]

FINLAY, JAMES, youngest son of James Finlay in Wallyford, East Lothian, died in Tobago on 10 September 1806. [SM.69.77]

FINLAY, Miss JANET, from Wallyford, East Lothian, died on Madeira on 10 November 1809. [ARM]

FINLAYSON, JOHN, born 1752, tenant in Goseland, died on 12 February 1811, husband of Mary Young, born 1751, died on 11 June 1815. [Drumelzier gravestone, Peebles-shire]

FLEMING, CATHERINE, eldest daughter of Reverend William Fleming in West Calder, Mid Lothian, married Reverend John Dalgleish [1812-1884], of New Amsterdam, Berbice, in Georgetown, Demerara, on 24 November 1869. [S.7934]

FLEMING, MATILDA, eldest daughter of Reverend David Fleming in Carriden, West Lothian, married James Edgar of Keithock, Lower Canada, on 9 July 1840. [AJ.4827]

FLICHTY, JAMES, born 1816, died 23 June 1890. [Eccles gravestone, Berwickshire]

FORD, or DUDGEON, ALISON, in New York, sister and heir of William Scott Ford, son of Peter Ford in Eyemouth, Berwickshire, also, heir to her sister Mary Ford, 1855. [NRS.S/H]

FORD, WILLIAM, son of John Ford an Excise officer at Coldstream, Berwickshire, was apprenticed to Archibald Gilchrist and Son, merchants in Edinburgh, foe five tears on 27 June 1799. [ERA]

FORDYCE, JOHN, eldest son of Thomas John Fordyce of Ayton, Berwickshire, Lieutenant Colonel of the 74th Highlanders, was killed at Watercloof, Cape of Good Hope, South Africa, on 6 November 1851. [FJ.994]

FORMAN, Mrs CHRISTIAN, widow of Thomas Broun an Excise officer and feuar in Duns, Berwickshire, testament, 1800, Comm. Lauder. [NRS]

FORREST, JAMES, a plasterer in Port Seton, East Lothian, in 1790. [NRS.JP2.6.3.1.22]

FORREST, JAMES, born 1796, died in New York on 24 January 1867, husband of Grace Scott, born 1799, died 3 March 1877. [Bathgate, Kirkton, gravestone, West Lothian]

FORREST, PATRICK, a merchant in Eyemouth, Berwickshire, testament, 1799, Comm. Lauder. [NRS]

FORREST, PETER, in Eyemouth Mill, Berwickshire, in 1834. [NRS.GD267.27.236.3646]

FORREST, ROBERT, from Dunbar, East Lothian, a minister ordained in Saltcoats on 27 February 1798, a minister in Saltcoats, Ayrshire, from 1798 until 1802, emigrated via Greenock aboard the Recovery bound for New York on 8 October 1802, settled in Stafford, Delaware County, New York, from 1810 until his death on 17 March 1846. [ANY][UPC]

FORRESTER, WILLIAM, an iron and brass founder in Bo'ness, West Lothian, was accused of poaching in 1825. [NRS.B48.16.6.6]

FORSYTH, or JAFFREY, ELIZABETH, a meal dealer in Duns, Berwickshire, testament, 1796, Comm. Lauder. [NRS]

FOWLES, WILLIAM, in Eyemouth Mill, Berwickshire, in 1834. [NRS.GD267.27.236.3646]

FRANCE, MARGARET, in Duns, Berwickshire, widow of Christopher Sligh a tenant in Buncle, Berwickshire, testament, 1790, Comm. Lauder. [NRS]

FRANCE, ROBERT, born 1827, son of Richard France, a tenant in Ninewells Mill, and his wife Isabella Wilson, died at Fenelon Falls, Canada West, on 25 February 1862. [Cockburnspath gravestone]

FRANK, AGNES, daughter of John Frank of Bughtrig, testament, 1796, Comm. Lauder. [NRS]

FRANK, CHARLES, of Boughbridge, born 1743, Captain of the Scots Brigade in the Service of the States General of Holland, died in 1791. [Eccles gravestone, Berwickshire]

FRANK, JAMES, of Boughbridge, a Captain in the Service of the East India Company, died at Vellore in 1797. [Eccles gravestone, Berwickshire]

FRANK, WILLIAM B., born 1735, son of James Frank of Boughbridge, a Colonel and Collector of New York, died 1810. [Eccles gravestone, Berwickshire]

FRASER, ALEXANDER, Sheriff Clerk of East Lothian, father of Simon Fraser who died in Gibsonport, Mississippi, on 23 October 1819. [EA.5853.423][AJ.3757][S.2.100]

FRASER, BAILEY SIMPSON, born 1808, late from New Orleans, Louisiana, died in Portobello, Mid Lothian, on 16 July 1861. [East Preston Street gravestone, Edinburgh]

FRASER, JAMES, born in Kelso, Roxburghshire, an indigo planter in Monghyr, Calcutta, Bengal, India, eldest son of Thomas Fraser, a merchant in Kelso, Roxburghshire, and his wife Mary Gray daughter of James Gray a brazier in Kelso, heir to his maternal aunt Mary Gray, 1827, [NRS.S/H]; died in Calcutta, India, on 16 April 1832. [South Park gravestone, Calcutta]

FRASER, JAMES, was accused of aiding the escape of Donald McCaul from Linlithgow Tolbooth, West Lothian, in 1822. [NRS.B48.16.6.4]

FRASER, JOHN, born 1789, son of Reverend John Fraser, [1753-1812], and his wife Jane Smith, [1765-1831], in Libberton, died in Jamaica at the residence of his uncle Dr Patrick Smith, on 6 November 1821. [Libberton gravestone, Mid Lothian]

FRASER, JOHN DENHOLM, a Stipendiary Magistrate in Demerara, youngest son of William Fraser in Melrose, Roxburghshire, married Johanna Bishop, daughter of Edward Bishop of Plantation Zorg, in Essequibo, on 22 May 1849. [EEC.21832]

FRASER, SIMON, son of Alexander Fraser the Sheriff Clerk of Haddingtonshire, died in Gibsonport, Mississippi, on 23 October 1819. [EA.5863.423]

FRASER, WALTER, from Falshope, Selkirkshire, a tailor in New York, married Jemima Carter in 1784, died in May 1793. [ANY]

FRENCH, JOHN, son of Thomas French in St Boswells, Roxburghshire, died in Charleston, South Carolina, in 1852. [S.22.9.1852]

FREW, ALEXANDER, born in 1794, died in Jamaica on 10 October 1826. [Kirkton, Bathgate, West Lothian]

FRIAR, JOHN, from Galashiels, Selkirkshire, a divinity student in 1829, settled in America as an agriculturalist. [AUPC]

GALLIE, ALEXANDER, born in 1839, second son of Thomas Gallie in East Linton, Haddington, East Lothian, died in Basse Terre, St Kitts on 16 November 1868. [S.7919]

GARDINER, RACHEL, daughter of Gilbert Gardiner, a joiner in Dunbar, East Lothian, spouse of John Colquhoun, a chairmaker in Edinburgh, a Process of Separation, in 1815. [NRS.CC8.6.1559]

GARDINER, THOMAS M., a farmer from Aberlady Bay, East Lothian, died in St Michael's, Hinchenbrook, Chateaugay, Canada West, in 1854. [S.13.5.1854]

GARDNER, ANDREW, in Duanscale, Trelawney, Jamaica, a disposition in favour of his brother Patrick Gardner, an Excise supervisor in Musselburgh, Mid Lothian, subscribed on 9 September 1797. [NRS.RD3.278.840]

GIBSON, ADAM, from Selkirk, died in America on 11 October 1861. [Inventory, 1862, Edinburgh, NRS]

GIBSON, JAMES TAYLOR, from Linlithgow, West Lothian, of the firm John Gibson and Company in New Orleans, Louisiana, died there on 12 February 1849. [SG.1804][W.XVII.1804]

GIBSON, JOHN, and his wife Jean Taylor, in Linlithgow, West Lothian, parents of James Taylor Gibson, born 8 October 1805, a merchant in New Orleans, Louisiana, died there on 12 February 1849. [SG.1804]

GIBSON, JOHN, a fish curer in Fisher Row Musselburgh, Mid Lothian, father of Robert Forrest Gibson, born in 1859, died in Rio de Janeiro, Brazil, on 21 March 1876. [S.10229]

GIBSON, JOHN, a Writer to the Signet, married Mary Ann Mazyck Weston, second daughter of Paul Weston of Charleston, South Carolina, in Portobello, Mid Lothian, on 10 April 1849. [SG.18.1810]

GIBSON, MARGARET DRYSDALE, born 8 May 1830, died in Buenos Ayres, Argentina, on 31 July 1896, buried in Chacanta, Buenos Ayres. [Preston Kirk gravestone, East Lothian]

GIFFORD, ANDREW, born 1761 in Loanhead, Mid Lothian, emigrated to New York as a cabinetmaker in 1784, a furniture manufacturer and timber merchant there, died on 28 November 1846. [ANY]

GILROY, RALPH, late of Jamaica, died in Gainslaw, Berwickshire, on 12 November 1825. [AJ.4063] [EEC.17815]

GLAISTER, ROBERT, born 1786, a veterinary surgeon in Kelso, died on 28 November 1828, husband of Mary Fishburn, born 1789, died On 28 May 1855. [Kelso gravestone, Roxburghshire]

GLASGOW, ROBERT, born 1745, a joiner and feuar in Leitholm, died 8 October 1800, husband of Agnes Whitehead, born 1756, died on 21 May 1840. [Eccles gravestone, Berwickshire]

GLASS, JOHN, in Newton of Balcanquhal, late from Jamaica, died in Portobello, Midlothian, on 30 January 1845. [EEC.21305]

GLASSELL, WILLIAM, probably from Haddington, East Lothian, settled in Fredericksburg, Virginia, by 1792. [Spotsylvania Deed Book N, 3 April 1792]

GLEN, GEORGE, son of John Glen, a farmer in Tranent, East Lothian, was apprenticed to John Crawford, a baker in Edinburgh, for five years on 14 March 1793. [ERA]

GLEN, WALTER, from Kirkliston, West Lothian, settled in Great Salt Lake City, Utah, nephew and heir to his uncle Walter Glen a merchant in Linlithgow, West Lothian, who died on 23 October 1855. [NRS.S/H]

GOLDIE, ALEXANDER, born 1804 in Midlothian, educated at Edinburgh University, minister of St Andrew's Presbyterian Church in Jamaica in 1846, died in Kingston on 22 July 1847. [F.7.669] [St Andrew's gravestone, Jamaica]

GOLDIE, THOMAS DICKSON, born 1799, sixth son of James Goldie in Bonnyrigg, Midlothian, died in Demerara on 1 December 1820. [BM.8.708] [EA]

GOODALL. GAVIN, in Galt, Canada West, married Janet Ainslie, daughter of William Ainslie, at Moat, Roslin, Mid Lothian, on 20 March 1862. [EEC.236.94]

GOODFELLOW, ALEXANDER, of Headshaw, Ashkirk, Roxburghshire, father of William Goodfellow who married Maggie Harrow, youngest daughter of John Harrow, from Paisley, Renfrewshire, in Buenos Ayres, Argentina, on 25 April 1873. [S.9326]

GOODLET, JANE, from Musselburgh, Mid Lothian, died in New York on 2 January 1836. [NRS.SC70.1.56]

GORDON, JAMES IRVING, of Carlton, born 1839, youngest son of Sir John Gordon of Earlston, Berwickshire, died 3 November 1862. [Earlston gravestone, Montego Bay, Jamaica]

GORDON, Sir JOHN, if Earlston, Berwickshire, married Julia Gallimore, daughter of Jervis Gallimore of Greenvale, in Water Valley, Jamaica, on 17 April 1811. [SM.73.957]

GOWDIE, FRANCIS, born 7 August 1747, son of Reverend John Gowdie and his wife Katherine Scott, a Major General in the Service of the East India Company in Madras, India, died 12 September 1813. [F.2.149]

GRAHAM, Dr ANDREW, in Dalkeith, Mid Lothian, father of Andrew Graham who died at Montego Bay, Jamaica, on 24 November 1828. [BM.25.682]

GRAHAM, ANDREW, son of William Graham, a master at Haddington Grammar School, East Lothian, was accused of mobbing and rioting there in 1831. [NRS.AD14.3358]

44

GRAHAM, HUGH, born 1755 at Slateheugh, West Calder, West Lothian, educated at Edinburgh University and at Theological Hall in Haddington, licenced as a minister in 1781, emigrated via Greenock to Halifax, Nova Scotia, in 1785, a minister in Cornwallis, N.S., from1785 to 1800, and in Stewiacke, Truro, N.S., from 1800 to his death in 1829. [HPC]

GRAHAM, JAMES, born in Jedburgh, Roxburghshire, formerly a forester on the Cromarty estate, died at Seamore, Garden Plantation, Jamaica, in August 1841. [AJ.4892]

GRAHAM, JOHN, born 5 November 1733 in Whitekirk, Dunbar, East Lothian, son of Reverend Alexander Pyot, [1700-1765], and his wife Eleanor Stevenson, died 1742, emigrated to Georgia in 1753, a planter, Lieutenant Governor of Georgia in 1776, a Loyalist, died in Naples in 1795. [Ga.Gaz.280][NRS.2.244/2.149; GD110.999/1046; GD105] [TNA.AO12.3.111, etc]

GRAY, ANDREW, a tinsmith in Edinburgh, John Gray a printer in Strabane, County Tyrone, Ireland, Stuart Gray a currier in Kelso, Roxburghshire, Robert Gray a tinsmith there, George Gray in Edinburgh, Alison Gray spouse of Richard Jack in Edinburgh, and Christian Gray widow of William Romanis a smith in Kelso, children of John Gray, coppersmith in Kelso, and his wife Helen Wylie, heirs to their grand-mother Alison Stuart widow of Gilbert Stuart a feuar and butcher in Kelso, 1826. [NRS.S/H]

GRAY, JANE, born 1830, daughter of John Gray in Lennel Newtown and his wife Janet Dodds, wife of Robert Douglas, died in Canada West on 26 July 1864. [Lennel gravestone, Berwickshire]

GRAY, JOHN, son of George Gray in Livingston, West Lothian, died in Jamaica in 1794. [SM][EA]

GRAY, Lieutenant JOHN, in Queensferry, West Lothian, testament, 1826, Comm. Edinburgh. [NRS]

GRAY, JOHN, eldest son of Thomas Gray in Duns, Berwickshire, died at the Rio Grande in South America, on 1 October 1841. [EEC.20315]

GRAY, JOHN, born 1820, son of John Gray in Lennel Newtown and his wife Janet Dodds, wife of Robert Douglas, died in Canada West on 22 January 1863. [Lennel gravestone, Berwickshire]

GRAY, PETER, born 1808, son of Peter Gray and his wife Marion Mason, died in Port Royal, Jamaica, on 12 April 1835. [Duns gravestone, Berwickshire]

GRAY, THOMAS, son of Matthew Gray a baker in Musselburgh, was apprenticed to Robert Middlemist, a baker in Edinburgh, for five years on 27 June 1799. [ERA]

GRAY, WALTER, born 1797 in Jedburgh, Roxburghshire, died in Madoc, Upper Canada, on 18 May 1846. [W.VII.695]

GRIEVE, ALEXANDER, a merchant in Greenlaw, Berwickshire, testament, 1795, Comm. Lauder. [NRS]

GRIEVE, HENRY, son of James Grieve tenant in Little Pinkerton, Dunbar, was apprenticed to James Inglis, a merchant in Edinburgh, for five years on 5 December 1791. [ERA]

GRIEVE, ISABELLA, born 1780, wife of John Hall, [1767-1843], died in Wisconsin on 13 January 1860. [Coldingham gravestone, Berwickshire]

GRIEVE, WALTER, born 1785, son of Reverend Walter Grieve, [1747-1822], and his wife Jean Ballantyne, [1741-1826], died in the West Indies on 19 September 1807. [Yarrow gravestone, Selkirkshire]

GRINDLAY, JAMES, a shipmaster in Bo'ness, West Lothian, son of Thomas Grindlay a shipmaster there, 1794. [NRS.S/H]

GRINTON, DAVID, a cabinet maker from Musselburgh, Mid Lothian, died in Morrisana Village, New York, in 1859. [CM.21737]

GROSART, JAMES, of High Street, Peebles, father of Alexander Grosart, born 1851, died in Toronto, Canada, on 10 October 1884. [S.12893]

HAGGARSTON, MARGARET FRANCES, wife of Lewis Eyre in Brussels, Belgium, heir to her great great grandfather William Robertson of Ladykirk, Berwickshire, who died on 25 April 1783, on 28 December 1852. [NRS.S/H]

HAGGARSTON, WINIFRED, a nun in St Andrew's Convent, in Belgium, heir to her great great grandfather William Robertson of Ladykirk, Berwickshire, who died on 25 April 1783, on 28 December 1852. [NRS.S/H]

HAIG, BARBARA, in The Villa Haig, Rome, sister and heir of James Haig of Bemersyde, Berwickshire, a Writer to the Signet, on 17 March 1858. [NRS.S/H]; an inventory, 1873. [NRS.SC70.164/27]

HAIG, JAMES, of Bemerside, Roxburghshire, son of James Haig there, heir to his cousin Isaac Haig of Third, Roxburghshire, 18 March 1794. [NRS.S/H]

HAIG, JAMES, a miller in Van Dieman's Land, [Tasmania], Australia, son and heir of Helen Haig at Coldstream Bridge Toll, Berwickshire, 1831. [NRS.S/H]

HAIG, MARY, in Italy, sister and heir of James Haig of Bemersyde, Berwickshire, a Writer to the Signet, on 17 March 1858. [NRS.S/H]; dead by 1871. [NRS.RD5.1417/304]

HAIG, ROBERT, born in Dunbar, East Lothian, died on 29 December 1819. [Old Scots gravestone, Charleston, South Carolina]

HAIG, SOPHIA, in Italy, sister and heir of James Haig of Bemersyde, Berwickshire, a Writer to the Signet, on 17 March 1858. [NRS.S/H]

HAIG, WILLIAM, third son of Anthony Haig of Bemerside, Roxburghside, and his wife Barbara Robertson, died in Martinique on 1 May 1794. [HB]

HALL, ALISON, widow of George Moffat a draper in USA, heir to her grandfather William Hall a smith in Kelso, Roxburghshire, 1850. [NRS.S/H]

HALL, GEORGE, born 1780 in Kelso, Roxburghshire, a merchant, was naturalised in South Carolina on 5 June 1812, died in 1824. [NARA.M1183-1] [Old Scots gravestone, Charleston]

HALL, ISABELLA, wife of W. Bennet in New York, heir to her grandfather William Hall a smith in Kelso, Roxburghshire, 1850. [NRS.S/H]

HALL, JAMES, born 1777 in Roslin, Mid Lothian, a stone-cutter in Charleston, South Carolina, was naturalised on 7 September 1813. [NARA.M1183.1]

HALL, JOHN, born 19 August 1785 in Roslin, Mid Lothian, was naturalised in South Carolina on 23 April 1824. [SCA. Misc. Records W4.405]

HALL, Sir JOHN, of Dunglass, born 16 September 1787, died on 2 April 1860, husband of Julia ....., born 1 November 1798, died on 3 October 1874. [Dunglass church mural, East Lothian]

HALL, JOHN, born 1829, son of John Hall and his wife Isabella Purves, died in Cleveland, Ohio, on 15 September 1852. [Swinton gravestone, Berwickshire]

HALL, JOHN, second son of Alexander Hall a wood merchant in Fisherrow, Midlothian, died in New York on 31 January 1845. [EEC.21219]

HALL, JULIAN, born 17 January 1837, fifth son of Sir John Hall of Dunglass, a Lieutenant General, of the Coldstream Guards from 1854 to 1881, fought at the Siege of Sebastipol in the Crimea, died on 15 August 1911. [Dunglass church mural, East Lothian]

HALL, THOMAS, a watchmaker, found guilty of swindling in Jedburgh, Roxburghshire, was sentenced to transportation to the colonies for seven years, in April 1790. [AJ.2207]

HALL, WILLIAM, born 1775 in Kelso, Roxburghshire, a merchant who was naturalised in Charleston, South Carolina, on 23 January 1804, died at the Sandy River, Chester District, S.C., on 29 April 1828, buried in the Columbia Presbyterian cemetery. [SCGaz.3.5.1828] [NARA.M1183.1]

HALLIDAY, THOMAS SCOTT, born 1853, from Bo'ness, West Lothian, died in Georgetown, Demerara, on 1 September 1881. [S.11919]; father of a daughter born in Georgetown on 18 December 1879. [S.11387]

HAMILTON, ALEXANDER JAMES, only son of the late James Hamilton of Ballincreiff, Linlithgow, West Lothian, in New York, subscribed to a deed there on 27 June 1800. [NRS.RD2.297.400]

HAMILTON, CLAUD, brother of Marion Hamilton in Portobello, Mid Lothian, of the Bank of Bengal at Mirzapore, India, 1853. [NRS.S/H]

HAMILTON, ROBERT, born on 14 September 1753, son of Reverend John Hamilton and his wife Jean Wight in Bolton, East Lothian, an entrepreneur and a Member of the Legislature of Ontario, died in Queenstown, Upper Canada, on 8 March 1809. [F.1.357] [DCB]

HAMILTON, THOMAS, probably from Kelso, Roxburghshire, later in Kingston, Jamaica, a deed, 1807. [NRS.RD5.389.42]

HAMILTON-DALRYMPLE, of North Berwick, East Lothian, family papers, from 1543 until 1875. [NRS.GD110]

HANDISYD, JAMES, in Kelso, Roxburghshire, a letter, 1825. [NRS.GD157.2662]

HARDIE, GEORGE, fifth son of Archibald Hardie a merchant in Bo'ness, West Lothian, died in Natchez, Georgia, on 7 September 1818. [S.97.18]

HARDIE, ROBERT, born 20 October 1805 in Hawick, Roxburghshire, son of John Hardie a farmer, was educated at Glasgow University, a minister in British Guina, died there on 24 October 1837. [F.7.675]

HARDIE, ROBERT, and Margaret Gillis, both from Midlothian, were married in Halifax, Nova Scotia on 28 September 1833. [HJ.30.9.1833]

HARKSON, ROGER, a weaver in Belhaven, East Lothian, was accused of rioting in Dunbar in 1816. [NRS.SC40.54.1.31]

HARVIE, ALEXANDER, a shoemaker in Linlithgow, West Lothian, was accused of prison breaking, in 1820. [NRS.AD14.20.258]

HARVIE, Reverend JOHN, died on 27 August 1816, husband of Rebecca Sandilands, born 1759, died on 26 April 1838. [Innerwick gravestone, East Lothian]

HASTIE, JEAN, daughter of Philip Hastie a farmer in Castle Moffat, East Lothian, versus Arthur Crow, an Excise Officer in the Canongate, Edinburgh, a Process of Divorce in 1805. [NRS.CC8.6.1224]

HAY, Lieutenant Colonel JOHN, from Musselburgh, Mid Lothian, in the Service of the East India Company, died 22 October 1839, an inventory, 1840, Edinburgh. [NRS]

HAY, THOMAS, born 1821 in Kelso, Roxburghshire, a tallow chandler in New York, died there on 17 July 1896. [ANY]

HAY, WILLIAM, probably from Duns, Berwickshire, at Talavera la Real, Spain, in 1809. [NRS.NRAS.2720, bundle 724]

HENDERSON, ALEXANDER, son of Captain Henderson of Morrison's Haven, West Lothian, died in Kingston, Jamaica, on 9 September 1797. [EEC.408]

49

HENDERSON, ALEXANDER, born 1742, a smith in Leith, died 3 July 1815, husband of Helen Nimmo, born 1744, died 25 August 1815. [South Leith gravestone]

HENDERSON, CHARLES MURRAY, born 2 April 1815, son of Reverend John Henderson and his wife Grace Bell in Tranent, East Lothian, a surgeon in Honourable East India Company Service. [F.1.397]

HENDERSON, DAVID, a merchant in Linlithgow, West Lothian, versus Andrew Gardner, a wright in Linlithgow, a Process of Scandal and Defamation in 1825. [NRS.CS8.6.19.81]

HENDERSON, FRANCIS CHARTERS, born 24 July 1808, son of Reverend John Henderson and his wife Grace Bell in Tranent, East Lothian, a surgeon in East India Company Service. [F.1.397]

HENDERSON, HENRY WATSON, born 1799, son of William Henderson and his wife Janet Watson, a merchant in Grahamstown, Cape of Good Hope, South Africa, died on 24 December 1834. [Currie gravestone, Mid Lothian]

HENDERSON, JOHN, minister of Queensferry, West Lothian, versus John Martin a merchant and magistrate there, a Process of Scandal in 1804. [NRS.CS8.6.1192]

HENDERSON, ROBERT, second son of John Henderson in Bo'ness, West Lothian, died in Barbados on 29 May 1798. [AJ.2640][EA.3610.79]

HENDERSON, FRANCIS, a clock and watchmaker, late in Musselburgh, Mid Lothian, then in Edinburgh, versus Janet Watson, daughter of Hugh Watson a weaver in Edinburgh, a Process of Divorce, 16 June 1790. [NRS.CC8.6.850]

HENDERSON, ROBERT, second son of John Henderson in Bo'ness, West Lothian, died in Barbados on 29 May 1798. [AJ.2640] [EA.3610.79]

HENDERSON, ROBERT, and Sons, shipowners in Bo'ness, West Lothian, in 1830. [NRS.GD2.73]

HENDERSON, THOMAS, born 1748, schoolmaster of Morham for 45 years, died on 22 January 1824, husband of Agnes Horsburgh, born 1766, died on 30 August 1838. [Morham gravestone, East Lothian]

HENDRY, GORDON, a carpenter in Dunbar, East Lothian, was accused of rioting in Dunbar in 1816. [NRS.SC40.54.1.32]

HENRICKS, JANE, in Eyemouth, Berwickshire, testament, 1795, Comm. Lauder. [NRS]

HENRY, JOHN, master of the Ann of Bo'ness trading between Greenock and Quebec in 1821. [NRS.E504.15.137]

HEPBURN, ALEXANDER, from Athelstaneford, East Lothian, emigrated via Greenock aboard the Portaferry to Quebec in May 1832. [QM.13.6.1832]

HEPBURN, WILLIAM, born 1782, a merchant in Prestonkirk, East Lothian, emigrated to New York aboard the George of New York on 12 August 1807. [TNA.PC1.3790]

HERCUS, GEORGE, born 1792 in Haddington, East Lothian, emigrated via Leith to Philadelphia, Pennsylvania, in July 1828, naturalised in Washington, D.C. in 1828. [NARA]

HERIOT, ALEXANDER H., and JAMES HERIOT, tenants in Ayton Law, later in Highlaws near Eyemouth, Berwickshire, in 1832. [NRS.CS238.H.12.64]

HERIOT, E. T., MD, possibly from Castle Mains, Dirleton, East Lothian, died at Mont Arena, Georgetown, South Carolina, on 22 November 1854. [W.XV.1608]

HERKES, JAMES, born in Innerwick, East Lothian, died in Halifax, Nova Scotia, on 6 May 1832. [Acadian Recorder, 12.5.1832]

HEUGH, THOMAS, a fisherman in Queensferry, West Lothian, subscribed to a bond of caution for John Ferguson and Thomas Henderson, fishermen in Queensferry in 1803. [NRS.CS271.746]

HEWAT, Dr ALEXANDER, born 1740, probably in Kelso, Roxburghshire, was educated at Edinburgh University, minister of the Scots Kirk in Charleston, South Carolina, from 1763 until 1775, a Loyalist who returned to Scotland, died in 1829 possibly in London. [F.7.663] [CEG] [TNA.AO12.47.428] [JSH.20.50]

HEWEIT, JAMES, born 1795, tenant in Sandy Knowe, died on 15 May 1854. [Kelso gravestone, Roxburghshire]

HILLS, JAMES, born in Berwickshire, settled in Savanna, Georgia, in 1804, died there on 17 July 1829. [Georgia Republican, 20.8.1829]

HILL, THOMAS, was granted a lease of Dean Bank in Eyemouth, Berwickshire, from 1821 to 1841. [NRS.267.27.239.3786/1]

HODGE, JAMES, a farmer in Cramond, West Lothian, 1819, nephew of David Hodge in New Orleans, Louisiana. [NRS.S/H]

HOGARTH, ROBERT, born 1735, a servant in Eccles Newtown,died 16 February 1825, husband of Isabel Alison, born 1742, died 15 November 1820. [Eccles gravestone, Berwickshire]

HOGG, ALEXANDER, a merchant in Eyemouth, Berwickshire, testament, 1795, Comm. Lauder. [NRS]

HOGG, ALEXANDER, born 1767, son of John Hogg, a tenant in Sisterpath Waulk Mill, and his wife Julia McLean, a surgeon in Charlestown, USA, died 1804. [Fogo gravestone, Berwickshire]

HOGG, ANDREW, son of William Hogg in Haddington, East Lothian, was educated at Marischal College in Aberdeen in 1835, later was a missionary in Jamaica. [MCA]

HOGG, JAMES, born 1730 in East Lothian, emigrated to North Carolina in 1774, a merchant and militiaman, settled at Cross Creek, Orange County, NC, died on 9 November 1805. [Hillsborough Presbyterian cemetery] [SM.67][Hogg pp, UNC]

HOGG, PETER, second son of Peter Hogg in Greenlaw, Berwickshire, died in Dominica in 1810. [EA.4864.95]

HOGG, ROBERT, youngest brother of the Ettrick Shepherd, died on passage to North America on 24 June 1831. [GM.103.286]

HOGG, WILLIAM, a baker in Dalkeith, Mid Lothian, a bond in 1822. [NRS.GD81.313]

HOGG, WILLIAM, born 1817, a mason, died in Leitholm on 1 October 1855, husband of Sarah Patterson, born 1815, died on 26 November 1881. [Eccles gravestone, Berwickshire]

HOGUE, THOMAS JOHN, from West Lothian, settled in Chittagong, Bengal, India, died 27 July 1844, inventory, 1845, Edinburgh. [NRS]

HOLDOM, RICHARD, in Gilmerton, Athelstaneford, East Lothian, a victim of theft and arson in 1849. [NRS. AD14 49.104]

HOME, ALEXANDER, a journeyman slater in Haddington, East Lothian, was accused of mobbing and rioting there in 1831. [NRS.AD14.3358]

HOME, AUGUSTA, eldest daughter of John Home of Homefield, Berwickshire, and wife of David James formerly a seed merchant in Dundee, died in Algiers, New Orleans, Louisiana, on 11 May 1867. [PJD.493]

HOME, GEORGE, of Branxton, was advised of the death of his brother Ninian Home in Grenada, during a slave uprising, in a letter from Patrick Home at Rappahannock Forge, Virginia, in 1795. Further letters between them in 1801, 1802, and 1803, refer to a Francis Hume in Virginia. [NRS.GD267.1.3]

HOME, JAMES, the distributor in the Stamp Office in Duns, Berwickshire, a ledger from 1827 to 1831. [NRS CS96.4234]

HOME, JOHN, son of William Home a brewer in Fisherrow, was apprenticed to John Morison, a barber in Edinburgh, for seven years on 31 March 1791. [ERA]

HOME, Mrs, wife of Ninian Home of Paxton, Berwickshire, died in Grenada in 1794. [SM.56.734]

HONEYMAN, THOMAS, of Veitch Park, Haddington, East Lothian, father of Isabella Wallace Honeyman who married James MacFadyen of the National Bank of Chile, at 233 Calle de Victoria in Valparaiso, Chile, in 1869. [S.8087]

HOOD, CHRISTIAN, born 1815, daughter of William Hood, died in Port Cook, Australia, in September 1852. [Duns gravestone, Berwickshire]

HOOD, GEORGE, born 1817, son of William Hood, died in Merang, Australia, in June 1859. [Duns gravestone, Berwickshire]

HOOD, JOHN, a corn merchant in Dunbar, papers, 1815. [NRS.CS40.20.43]

HOOD, MARK COCKBURN COSSAR, born 1849, youngest son of George Hood tenant of Greendykes, Berwickshire, died at Corladdy Station, Upper Porar River, Queensland, Australia, on 18 May 1876. [AJ.6723]

HOOD, PETER, born 1812, son of James Hood and his wife Jean Kemp, died in New Plymouth, North Island, New Zealand, on 26 July 1856. [Coldingham gravestone, Berwickshire]

HOPE, CHARLES JAMES, son of Robert Hope in Fenton Barns, East Lothian, settled in Hamilton, Ontario, letters, 1837-1878. [NRS.RH1.2.612]

HOPE, JAMES, a mason in Morebattle, Roxburghshire, grandfather of James Hope in Geelong, Port Philip, New South Wales, Australia, 1851. [NRS.S/H]

HOPE, Dr JOHN, died in Demerara on 12 August 1804. [West Linton gravestone, Peebles-shire]

HOPE, JOHN, from Galashiels, Selkirkshire, a member of the Scots Charitable Society of Boston, New England, in 1819. [NEHGS]

HOPE, MARY, born 1786, wife of Andrew Weal late Baron officer to the Duke of Buccleugh, died in Flamboro West. Canada West, in 1848. [W.604]

HOPKIRK, GEORGE, born 1765, son of Alexander Hopkirk and his wife Jean Briggs in Dryburgh, died at Roxburgh Castle, Jamaica, on 11 March 1813. [Dryburgh Abbey gravestone, Roxburghshire] [EA.5159.13]

HORSBURGH, ALEXANDER, of that Ilk and Pirn, born 1789, a Lieutenant Colonel of the 46th Regiment, of Bengal Native Infantry, died on 26 January 1865, husband of Helen Hay McLaren, born 1804, died on 17 January 1901. [Kailzie gravestone, Peebles-shire]

HORSBRUGH, THOMAS, of that Ilk and Pirn, formerly a Captain of the 9th Dragoons, died in 1852. [Kailzie gravestone, Peebles-shire]

HORSBURGH, WILLIAM, born 1731, a resident of Morham, died on 26 September 1806, husband of Margaret Skirving, born 1731, died on 21 February 1814. [Moreham gravestone, East Lothian]

HOSIE, GEORGE, born 1776, son of George Hosie and his wife Janet Gregg, died at Davies Cove, Jamaica, in 1800. [Abercorn gravestone, West Lothian]

HOW, ROBERT NESBIT, born 1799 in Berwick, settled in Georgetown district, South Carolina, was naturalised in Charleston, S.C., on 8 December 1821. [NARA.M1183.1]

HOWE, WILLIAM, son of Reverend William Howe, minister at Skirling, Peebles-shire, was apprenticed to John Spottiswood, a merchant and ironmonger in Edinburgh, for five years on 1 March 1792. [ERA]

HOW, THOMAS, born 1801 in Berwick on Tweed, Northumberland, applied to become a citizen of South Carolina, on 11 October 1823. [NARA.M1183.1]

HOWDEN, ALEXANDER, son of Alexander Howden a tenant in East Fortune, East Lothian, was apprenticed to David Paterson, an insurance broker and banker in Edinburgh, for five years on 4 August 1796. [ERA]

HOY, WILLIAM, a portioner in Gattonside, Roxburghshire, heir to his grandfather William Hoy a portioner there, 4 April 1793. [NRS.S/H]

HUGGIN, WILLIAM, born 1810, died 17 May 1869, husband of Eizabeth Rutherford, born 1814, died 7 September 1876. [Spott gravestone, East Lothian]

HUME, ALEXANDER, born 23 June 1819, fifth son of James Hume the pilot in Granton, Mid Lothian, died in India on 6 July 1847. [St Stephen's gravestone, Dum Dum, Bengal]

HUME, DAVID, in Tennessee, son and heir of George Hume a shoemaker in Lauder, Berwickshire, 1838. [NRS.S/H]

HUME, ROBERT, youngest son of Alexander Hume at Coldingham Law, Berwickshire, died in Bagnals, St Mary's, Jamaica, on 12 January 1804. [SM.66.479] [GM.74.596]

HUME, ROBERT, son of William Hume a weaver in Linlithgow, West Lothian, was apprenticed for 4 years to Robert Henderson and Sons shipowners in Bo'ness, West Lothian, an indenture dated 1830. [NRS.GD2.73; GD5.280]

HUNTER, HECTOR ALEXANDER, a farmer and smith in Lower Canada, grandson and heir of John Hunter a smith in Linlithgow, West Lothian, who died before 1810. [NRS.S/H]

HUNTER, HECTOR, with his wife and four children, from Berwick-on-Tweed, emigrated via Greenock aboard the Portaferry to Quebec in May 1832. [QM.13.6.1832]

HUNTER, HELEN, in Lilliesleaf, Roxburghshire, relict of John Cockburn in Belses, heir to her brother John Turnbull a tailor and portioner of Lilliesleaf, 1845. [NRS.S/H]

HUNTER, HELEN, wife of Mark Hermiston sr. in Camden, Upper Canada, heir to her maternal uncle John Turnbull a tailor and portioner of Lilliesleaf, Roxburghshire, 1845. [NRS.S/H]

HUNTER, JAMES, a writer in Duns, Berwickshire, a letter in 1831. [NRS.267.27.250.4053]

HUNTER, JAMES, in North America, nephew and heir of Jane Hunter or Amos in Melrose, Roxburghshire, 1839. [NRS.S/H]

HUNTER, JENNET, born 1806, wife of John Jeffrey late of Yetholm, Roxburghshire, died in Hope township, Barry County, Michigan, in 1873. [GH.10520]

HUNTER, JOHN, a smith in Linlithgow, West Lothian, dead by 1810. [NRS.S/H]

HUNTER, JOHN, born 1787 in Tranent, East Lothian, a carpenter, died in St John, New Brunswick, on 13 December 1831. [New Brunswick Courier, 17.12.1831]

HUNTER, JOHN ALEXANDER, born 1820, died near Vizianagram in the East Indies, on 9 July 1848. [Innerwick gravestone, East Lothian]

HUNTER, JOHN, born 1847, son of Daniel Hunter, died in Galt, Canada, on 12 February 1883, [Stenton gravestone, East Lothian]

HUNTER, MAY GREY, third daughter of General Martin Hunter of Anton's Hill, Berwickshire, died in Rome, Italy, on 14 February 1855. [Protestant Cemetery, Rome]

HUNTER, RICHARD, third son of James Hunter of Thurston, born 15 July 1816, Lieutenant Colonel of the 7th Madras Cavalry, India, died in St Jean de Luz, France, on 8 July 1885. [Innerwick gravestone, East Lothian]

HUNTER, ROBERT FRANCIS, born 1815, Major of the 71st Regiment, Highland Light Infantry, died at Kertch in the Crimea on 30 October 1855, interred at Yenikale. [Innerwick gravestone, East Lothian]

HUTCHISON, JAMES, a prisoner in Dunbar, East Lothian, accused of sheep stealing in 1816. [NRS.AD14.16.65]

HUTTON, JAMES, a sloop-master in Cramond, West Lothian, testament, 1825, Comm. Edinburgh. [NRS]

HUTTON, WILLIAM, a baker in South Queensferry, West Lothian sequestration, 1840. [NRS.CS280.30.52]

HYND, JOHN, a collier at Ballencrieff Toll, Bathgate, West Lothian, a petition in 1823. [NRS.B48.16.6.4]

HYNDMAN, ALEXANDER, in Joppa, Midlothian, applied to settle in Canada on 2 March 1815. [NRS.RH9]

IMERY, JAMES, born 1809, son of William Imery, [1782-1860], feuar in Ploughhead, and his wife Isobel Short, [1781-1843], died in the West Indies in 1843. [Greenlaw gravestone, Berwickshire]

INGLIS, JAMES, lately in Kingston, Jamaca, died in Musselburgh, Midlothian, on 3 October 1823. [DPCA.1107]

INGLIS, THOMAS, born 1834 in Galashiels, Selkirkshire, son of George Adam Inglis and his wife Isabella Gray, settled in Detroit, Michigan. [Galashiels gravestone]

INGRAM, ANDREW, born 1773 in Eyemouth, Berwickshire, a ships carpenter, was admitted as a citizen of South Carolina on 12 December 1803. [NARA.M1183.1]

INGRAM, JAMES, born 1812, died on 15 April 1895, husband of Agnes Scoular, born 12 December 1817, died on 4 February 1882. [Drumelzier gravestone, Peebles-shire]

INNES, DAVID KENNEDY, born 1843, son of David Innes and his wife Elisabeth Stephens, died in Wyoming on 15 August 1878. [Lennel gravestone, Berwickshire]

INNES, GILBERT, of Stow, Peebles-shire, letters from 1805 to 1806. [NRS.GD113.5.455]

INNES, JOHN, of Cowie, born 1776, died in Portobello, Mid Lothian, in 1832. [AJ.17.4.1832]

INSTANT, KELMAN, a skipper in North Berwick, East Lothian, testament, 1824, Comm. Edinburgh. [NRS]

ISAAC, JOHN JENKINS, born 1837, second son of James Isaac, died in Sloonfield on the MacQuarrie River, Australia, on 9 July 1862. [Melrose gravestone, Roxburghshire]

JACK, JOHN, in East Mains, Lauder, Berwickshire, father of George John Jack, born 1853, died in Georgetown, Demerara, on 3 January 1881. [S.12029]

JACKSON, HENRY, eldest son of .... Jackson in Musselburgh, Mid Lothian, died in New York on 2 February 1849. [SG.18.1830] [EEC.21825]

JACKSON, PETER, from Musselburgh, Mid Lothian, factor of the Staple at Veere, Zeeland, in 1791. [NRS.S/H]

JAFFREY, JAMES, born 1803, a bookseller from Berwick-on-Tweed, died in Galt, Ontario, on 20 October 1884. [S.12901]

JAFFREY, JOHN, guilty of writing a threatening letter, was sentenced at Jedburgh, Roxburghshire, to seven years transportation to the colonies in 1815. [NRS.GD1.959]

JAMESON, JAMES WARDROPE, in Genoa, Italy, son and heir of his parents William Jameson and his wife Elizabeth Jane Turnbull in Portobello, Midlothian, in 1851. [NRS.S/H]

JAMIESON, JOHN, formerly a merchant in Savannah, Georgia, a Loyalist in 1776, [TNA.AO12.51.266, etc]; but by 1794 a resident of Coats, Haddington, East Lothian, a deed. [NRS.RD3.279.116]

JAMIESON, JOHN, from Kelso, Roxburghshire, was admitted as a citizen of Rotterdam, Holland, on 29 September 1792. [RA]

JAMIESON, WILLIAM, and his wife Elizabeth Jane Turnbull in Portobello, Mid Lothian, parents of James Wardrope Jamieson, in Genoa, Italy, and Thomas Jamieson, a surgeon in Guayaguil, Ecuador, 1851. [NRS.S/H]

JARDINE, HENRY, born 12 March 1803, son of Sir Henry Jardine and his wife Catherine Skene, from Midlothian, died in Rome, Italy, on 11 January 1840. [Protestant Cemetery, Rome] [SGS]

JARDINE, WALTER, born in 1806, late in Jamaica, died in Lilliesleaf, Roxburghshire, on 19 September 1837. [Lilliesleaf gravestone]

JEFFREY, ANDREW, born 1809, died in Leitholm on 11 May 1874, husband of Agnes Robertson. [Eccles gravestone, Berwickshire]

JERDAN, JOHN, a bailie of Kelso, Roxburghshire, heir to his father John Jerdan a tanner and feuar there, 23 December 1790. [NRS.S/H]

JOHNSON, ROBERT, a house painter, second son of Robert Johnson in Duns Berwickshire, died in Duns Castle, St George, Jamaica, on 13 March 1809. [SM.71.478]

JOHNSON, WILLIAM, a Captain of the Royal Navy, son of William Johnson of Petterlaw and Foulden, Berwickshire, died in Georgina, Upper Canada, on 28 March 1851. [FJ.959]

JOHNSTON, ALEXANDER, born 1744, a blacksmith, died on 24 December 1805, husband of Elspeth Kemp, born 1740, died 25 December 1804. [Garvald gravestone, East Lothian]

JOHNSTON, or HENDERSON, ALISON, in Portobello, Mid Lothian, mother of George Henderson in New South Wales, 1850. [NRS.S/H]

JOHNSTON, ANDREW, a printer in Kelso, Roxburghshire, brother and heir of Margaret Johnston there, 1843. [NRS.S/H]

JOHNSTON, ARCHIBALD, a surgeon, son of John Johnston a writer in Bathgate, West Lothian, died in Berbice in December 1806. [SM.69.638]; his eldest daughter Margaret Johnstone, died there on 26 January 1820. [BM.9.121]

JOHNSTON, DAVID, born 1780 in Linlithgow, West Lothian, former soldier of the Royal Lanarkshire Militia, married Janet Jamieson, born 1782 in Linlithgow, then residing in Leith, applied to settle in Canada on 8 May 1827. [TNA.CO384.5.901]

JOHNSTON, FRANCIS, a surgeon, son of Reverend Andrew Johnston in Salton, East Lothian, died on Plantation Lusiquail, Demerara, on 28 July 1830. [S.1121]

JOHNSTONE, GEORGE, born 2 November 1780, son of Reverend Laurence Johnstone and his wife Esther Lauriston, in Earlston, Berwickshire, staff surgeon of the Connaught Rangers, died in Corfu, Greece, in 1833. [F.2.149]

JOHNSTON, Lady GEORGINA COCHRANE, third daughter of the Earl of Hopetoun, wife of Cochrane Johnstone the Governor of Dominica, died in Rosseau, Dominica, on 17 September 1797. [AJ.2608][EEC.418] [GM.67.1069]

JOHNSTON, HENRY, son of David Johnston in Corstorphine, Midlothian, was apprenticed to Benjamin Bell, a surgeon apothecary in Edinburgh, for five years, on 6 January 1791. [ERA]

JOHNSTON, JAMES, son of James Johnston a vintner in Dalkeith, Midlothian, was apprenticed to Francis Buchan and David Hunter, merchants in Edinburgh, for five years, on 25 October 1792. [ERA]

JOHNSTON, JAMES, born 1797, son of Walter Johnston in Joppa, Portobello, Midlothian, died in Leghorn/Livorno, Italy, on 20 May 1817. [SM.79.480]

JOHNSTONE, JAMES, in New York, nephew and heir of Captain A. Johnstone in Portobello, Mid Lothian, 1849. [NRS.S/H]

JOHNSTON, JOSEPH, son of Adam Johnston in Crossrig, [1749-1828], and his wife Janet Brown, [1759-1817], died in America. [Whitsome gravestone, Berwickshire]

JOHNSTON, PETER, born 1794 in Duns, Berwickshire, emigrated to Savannah, Georgia, in November 1819, was naturalised in Chester, South Carolina, on 18 October 1836. [Chester Naturalisations, B.60]

JOHNSTON, PETER, a contractor in Bo'ness, West Lothian, father of Agnes Johnston, born 1856, wife of David Stewart a joiner, died in St Andrews, Indiana, on 29 November 1882. [S.12301]

JOHNSTON, ROBERT, a housepainter, second son of Robert Johnston in Duns, Berwickshire, died at Duns Castle, St George, Jamaica, on 13 March 1809. [SM.71.478]

JOHNSTON, ROBERT, born 1791, son of Robert Johnston, [1760-1838], a weaver in Greenlaw, and his wife Isobel Black, [1759-1813], died in America in January 1830. [Greenlaw gravestone, Berwickshire]

JOHNSTON, WALTER, a sailor in Fisherrow, Midlothian, in 1790. [NRS.S/H]

JOHNSTON, WILLIAM, a farmer from Stobo, Peebles-shire, with Janet his wife, and one child, emigrated via Greenock to Canada in 1815. [TNA.CO385.2]

KARR, ANDREW SETON, eldest son of Daniel Seton, sometime in the service of the East India Company, second son of Daniel Seton, a merchant in Edinburgh, and his wife Jean Ramsay, heir to his grand-uncle Andrew Ramsay Karr of Kippilaw, 1821. [NRS.S/H]

KARR, ANDREW SILVER, of Kippilaw, died in France on 22 July 1833, inventory, 1834, Edinburgh. [NRS]

KAY, ROBERT, in Jamaica, brother and heir of Isabella Kay, daughter of John Kay, a feuar in Duns, Berwickshire, in 1841. [NRS.S/H]

KAY, Captain, master of the Lady Emma of Cockenzie, East Lothian, bound from Port Glasgow to Port Elliot, South Australia, landed there on 17 January 1855. [LCL.4392]

KEDGLIE, or KERVAND, ANN ELIZABETH, in America, daughter and heir of John Kedglie a slater from Tranent, East Lothian, later in Washington, in 1846. [NRS.S/H]

KEDGLIE, HENRY TURNBULL, in Tranent, East Lothian, son and heir of John Kedglie a slater from Tranent, East Lothian, later in Washington, DC, who died 14 July 1847. [NRS.S/H]

KEDGLIE, JOHN, born 1792 in East Lothian, emigrated via Liverpool to New York in December 1807, was naturalised in Washington, D.C., in 1839. [NARA]

KEIR, JOHN, Captain of the Royal Linlithgow Volunteers, was admitted as a burgess and guilds-brother of Dunfermline, Fife, on 15 August 1804. [DM]

KEIR, JOHN a weaver in Belhaven, East Lothian, was accused of rioting in Dunbar, East Lothian, in 1816. [NRS.SC40.54.1.31]

KELLIE, JOHN J., from Haddington, East Lothian, died in Vanleckhill, Canada West, on 12 January 1855. [EEC.22700]

KELLIE, MARY, a servant in Dunbar, East Lothian, a precognition into her death in 1820. [NRS.AD14.20.50]

KELLOCK, GEORGE, born 1800, eldest son of Alexander Kellock, MD, in Berwick-on-Tweed, Northumberland, a special magistrate, died in Leguan, Demerara, on 12 January 1839. [EEC.19872]

KEMP, EUPHEMIA, wife of Charles Francis Edwards in Canada, heir to her mother Mary Gibson, wife of David Kemp, a chemist in Portobello, Mid Lothian, who died on 24 June 1875. [NRS.S/H]

KEMP, HENRY, born 10 December 1814 in Musselburgh, Mid Lothian, settled in New York in the 1840s, died on 16 May 1898. [ANY]

KEMP, RICHARD, born 1786 in Haddington, East Lothian, an innkeeper at the Fishmarket there, was accused of mobbing and rioting there in 1831. [NRS.AD14.3358]

KENNAWAY, DAVID, was accused of a murder at Old Crosskeys Close, Dalkeith, Mid Lothian, in 1825. [NRS.AD14.25.6]

KENNEDY, Dr CHARLES, a physician in St Croix, Danish West Indies, married Margaret Cooper, daughter of Arthur Cooper in St Croix, in Eyemouth, Berwickshire, in October 1797. [EEC.392]

KENNEDY, THOMAS, from Hawick, Roxburghshire, emigrated via Greenock aboard the Portaferry to Quebec in May 1832. [QM.13.6.1832]

KERR, ALEXANDER, son of John Kerr a merchant in Dunbar, East Lothian, was apprenticed to Francis Sheills a baker in Edinburgh on 10 June 1790. [ERA]

KERR, ANDREW, born on 6 September 1754 in Kelso, Roxburghshire, died on 20 October 1820. [Old Scots gravestone, Charleston, South Carolina]

KERR, CHARLES, a Writer to the Signet, heir to his father Patrick Kerr of Abbotsrule, Roxburghshire, W.S., 18 June 1792, and to his mother Jean Hay, daughter of Thomas Hay of Huntingdon a Senator of the College of Justice, 5 July 1792. [NRS.S/H]

KERR, EDWARD, an innkeeper in Broxburn, West Lothian, was a victim of assault in 1823. [NRS.B48.16.6.4]

KERR, FRANCIS, born 1817, son of Thomas Kerr and his wife Margaret Walker, died in Cuba on 20 January 1843. [Athelstaneford gravestone, East Lothian]

KERR, GIBSON, a feuar in Yetholm, Roxburghshire, a bond of caution, 1803. [NRS.CS271.847]

KERR, ISABELLA, eldest daughter of Reverend Alexander Kerr in Stobo, Peebles-shire, married James Kerr, a Judge of the Courts of King's Bench and Vice Admiralty of Quebec, in Queen Street, Edinburgh, on 17 September 1818. [S.88.18]; their son was born in Quebec on 2 January 1820. [BM.7.118]; she died in Quebec on 29 March 1821. [BM.9.245]

KERR, JANE, daughter of Robert Kerr, a surgeon in Portobello, Mid Lothian, married Robert Haldane the Mexican Consul, in Carthagena, Columbia, on 24 July 1827. [BM.22.766]

KERR, ROBERT, a surgeon in Portobello, Mid Lothian, father of Jane Kerr who married Robert Haldane the Mexican Consul, in Carthagena, Columbia, on 24 July 1827. [BM.22.766]

KERR, ROBERT, of Chatto, Roxburghshire, died in Nice, France, on 6 December 1831, inventory, 1832, Edinburgh. [NRS]

KER, THOMAS, youngest son of Gilbert Ker of Gateshaw, died in Jamaica on 6 August 1821. [S.5.247]

KETCHEN, THOMAS, from Howgate, Midlothian, a theological student in 1810, later a minister in South Carolina. [UPC]

KIDD, ALEXANDER, born 1781, a cartwright from Blackburn, West Lothian, with wife Christian White born 1781, Alexander born 1805, Christian born 1806, Ann born 1807, William born 1809, Walter born 1810, James born 1812, and Eliza born 1815, applied to settle in Canada on 2 March 1815, emigrated via Greenock to Ontario in July 1815. [TNA.AO3; CO385.2][NRS.RH9]

KIDD, WILLIAM, a shoemaker in Linlithgow, West Lothian, was accused of robbery in 1823, a petition. [NRS.B48.16.6.4]

KING, ANN, born 1801, wife of George Paterson a cooper and fishcurer in Cockburnspath and in Dunbar, died 8 December 1847. [Cockburnspath gravestone, Berwickshire]

KING, JOHN, a farmer in Stamford, New York, brother and heir of William King, a stocking maker in Denholm, Roxburghshire, 1847. [NRS.S/H]

KING, JOHN, in Delaware, brother and heir of James King in Denholm, Roxburghshire who died 24 February 1872. [NRS.S/H]

KINGHORN, DAVID, born 1800 in Haddington, East Lothian, a wright in Northam, Haddington, was accused of mobbing and rioting there in 1831. [NRS.AD14.3358]

KINGHORN, WILLIAM, a miller in Schenectady, New York, grandson and heir of Robert McLaren a tailor in Chirnside, Berwickshire, 1851. [NRS.S/H]

KINLEYSIDE, PETER, born 1812, son of John Kinleyside, [1780-1861], and his wife Hellen Thompson, [1779-1851], died in California on 27 January 1857. [Whitsome gravestone, Berwickshire]

KINLEYSIDE, ROBERT, born 1814, son of John Kinleyside, [1780-1861], and his wife Hellen Thompson, [1779-1851], died in Labrador on 14 January 1850. [Whitsome gravestone, Berwickshire]

KIRTON, JOHN, son and heir of Barbara Anderson of Tushielaw, widow of Alexander Kirton in Barbados, who died in November 1790. [NRS.S/H]

KITCHEAN, JAMES, born 25 December 1797, a minister in Belleville, Canada, in 1831, died in Mordington, Berwickshire, on 30 November 1871. [Mordington gravestone]

KNOX, WILLIAM, possibly from Selkirk, emigrated, with his family, via Liverpool aboard the Republic bound for New York in 1838, a letter. [NRS.GD1.813.15]

LAIDLAW, ADAM, born 10 September 1810, son of William Laidlaw, [1760-1835], in Horsburgh Castle, Peebles-shire, and his wife Sarah Anderson, [1780-1827], died in Morpeth, Canada, on 13 May 1855. [Innerleithen gravestone, Peebles-shire]

LAIDLAW, JOHN, born 1794 in Roxburghshire, with his wife Agnes, born 1794 in Edinburgh, both teachers, emigrated via Leith to America, settled in Brooklyn, New York, naturalised there on 24 July 1820. [NARA]

LAIDLAW, or SOMMERVILLE, Mrs MARGARET, relict of Archibald Sommerville a surgeon in Lauder, Berwickshire, only child of Nicol Laidlaw, portioner of Newtoun, eldest son of Mungo Laidlaw, portioner there, eldest son of James Laidlaw, portioner there, eldest son of William Laidlaw, portioner there, was served heir to the said William Laidlaw her great-great-grandfather, 16 May 1794. [NRS.S/H]

LAIDLAW, ROBERT, son of James Laidlaw tenant in Hindleshope, died in Grenada on 2 August 1797. [EEC.372] [GM.67.897]

LAIDLAW, ROBERT, born 3 December 1813, son of William Laidlaw, [1760-1835], in Horsburgh Castle, Peebles-shire, and his wife Sarah Anderson, [1780-1827], died in Raleigh, Canada, on 25 April 1847. [Innerleithen gravestone, Peebles-shire] [EEC.21502]

LAIDLAW, WALTER, in Bombay, India, son and heir of William Laidlaw, a grocer in Hawick, Roxburghshire, 1854. [NRS.S/H]

LAIDLAW, WILLIAM, born 1760, tenant of Horsburgh Castle, died in Peebles on 3 October 1835, husband of Sarah Anderson, born 1780, died on 27 September 1827, father of Adam Laidlaw, born 10 September 1810, died in Morpeth, Canada, on 13 May 1855, also of Robert Laidlaw, born 3 December 1813, died in Raleigh, Canada, on 25 April 1847. [Innerleithen gravestone, Peebles-shire]

LAING, Captain JAMES, born 1768 in Grangemouth, West Lothian, died in St John, New Brunswick, on 17 September 1846. [W.VII.730]

LAING, ROBERT, and his wife Anne Jesson, from Berwickshire, settled in Peterborough County, Ontario, in 1810. [SG.32.3]

LAING, WILLIAM, and his wife Helen Mabon, from Berwickshire, settled in Peterborough County, Ontario, in 1810. [SG.32.3]

LAING, WILLIAM, was accused of poaching in Dalkeith Park, Mid Lothian, in 1823. [NRS.JC26.1823.197]

LAMB, ADAM, a shoemaker in Kelso, Roxburghshire, versus John Purves, a tailor there, re the theft of a game cock, in 1816. [NRS.AD30.17]

LAMB, JAMES, a builder in Aberlady, East Lothian, father of Peter Lamb who died in Aurora, USA, on 19 April 1877. [EC.28897]

LAMB, ROBERT HENRY, in Annawan, Illinois, son and heir of William Lamb jr. a nursery man in Galashiels, Selkirkshire, who died on 9 October 1856. [NRS.S/H]

LANDELL, GEORGE RICHARDSON, born 1785, a Lieutenant of the Royal Marines, died in Montreal, Quebec, on 8 August 1834, son of Reverend James Landell in Coldingham, Berwickshire. [Coldingham gravestone]

LANDELL, JAMES, born 9 November 1786, son of Reverend James Landell and his wife Janet Heriot, a Lieutenant of the 60th Regiment of Foot, died in Port Antonio, Jamaica, on 26 July 1803. [Coldingham gravestone, Berwickshire]

LANDELLS, JOHN, in Billie, Berwickshire, testament, 1799, Comm. Lauder. [NRS]

LANDELL, JOHN, brother of Reverend James Landell in Coldingham, Berwickshire, died in St Thomas, West Indies, in October 1809. [EA]

LANDELL, ROBERT, born 1838, son of William Landell, farmer of Coldingham Fleurs, died in Kingston, Jamaica, on 1 April 1866. [Foulden gravestone, Berwickshire]

LANDELL, THOMAS, born 1786, son of Reverend James Landell and his wife Janet Heriot, died in Jamaica on 25 November 1815. [Coldingham gravestone, Berwickshire]

LANDELL, WILLIAM, in Dalkeith, Mid Lothian, brother and heir of Robert Landell in Kingston, Jamaica, who died on 1 April 1866. [NRS.S/H]

LANG, JOHN, the Sheriff Clerk of Selkirkshire, son and heir to Andrew Lang a writer in Selkirk who died 10 November 1842, 1847. [NRS.S/H]

LANG, JOHN SIBBALD, an Ensign of the 94th Regiment, second son of John Lang the sheriff clerk of Selkirkshire, was killed at the storming of Badajoz, Spain, on 6 April 1812. [SM.74.479]

LAUDER, ALEXANDER, born 1796, eldest son of John Lauder of the Queen's Head Inn in Kelso, Roxburghshire, died in Jamaica on 17 January 1823. [DPCA.1076] [EEC.17424]

LAUDER, JAMES, born 1786, farmer in Northrig, died on 1 May 1847, husband of Elisabeth Morrison, born 1793, died in Barney Mains on 11 April 1865. [Morham gravestone, East Lothian]

LAUDER, JOHN, born in 1780, of the Royal Artillery, died in Guadaloupe, on 20 October 1815, husband of Isabella Penny, born 1788, died 13 January 1810. [Foulden gravestone, Berwickshire]

LAUDER, WILLIAM, son of John Lauder, a blacksmith in Whitelie, St Boswells, Roxburghshire, was victim of assault in 1849. [NRS.AD14.249.206]

LAW, JAMES, from Belhaven, East Lothian, applied to settle in Canada on 26 February 1815. [NRS.H9]

LAW, WILLIAM, [1827-1890], a forester in Bowland, Roxburghshire, and his wife Ann Richardson, [1830-1901], parents of William Law, born 1853, who died in Sao Paulo, Brazil, on 24 August 1887. [Lilliesleaf gravestone, Roxburghshire]

LAW, WILLIAM, only son of Reverend John Law in Innerleithen, Peebles-shire, died in Port of Spain, Trinidad, on 21 August 1855. [FE.9] [EEC.322794]

LAWRIE, SARAH A., born 1839, from Dalkeith, Midlothian, died and was buried in the British Cemetery, Funchal, Madeira, on 3 July 1872. [ARM]

LAWSON, CHARLOTTE, wife of Reverend George Brodie in Port of Spain, Trinidad, daughter and heir of George Lawson a minister in Selkirk, who died 15 December 1849. [NRS.S/H]

LAWSON, ROBERT, in South Vennel, Fisher Row, Musselburgh, Mid Lothian, father of James Lawson, an engineer, who died in Cera, Brazil, on 21 March 1874. [S.9687]

LEADBETTER, GEORGE, Quarter Master Sergeant of the Berwickshire Militia, in Coldstream, Berwickshire, son and heir of Alexander Leadbetter a merchant in Kelso, Roxburghshire, 1831. [NRS.S/H]

LEADBETTER, JAMES, born 1752, a merchant in Kelso, died on 6 January 1832, husband of Dorothea Richardson, born 1753, died on 17 November 1820. [Kelso gravestone, Roxburghshire]

LEARMONTH, JANE, born 1825, wife of James Cockburn, from Merton, Berwickshire, died in Daylesford, Victoria, Australia, on 2 April 1885. [S.13061]

LEARMONT, JOHN, in Georgia, son and heir of Marion Martin, wife of John Learmont in Welldale of Troquier, who died 8 September 1848. [NRS.SH]

LECK, HENRY, born 1784 in Morebattle, Roxburghshire, married Mary Kirkwood in 1812, settled in Nova Scotia in 1817. [SG.28.3.148]

LECKIE, JOHN, eldest son of Reverend Thomas Leckie in Peebles, died in New York on 22 August 1841. [AJ.4889]

LEGGAT, JANET, wife of Charles Buol in Philadelphia, Pennsylvania, heir to her great grandfather Andrew Leggat in Howdenburn, Hawick, Roxburghshire, who died 29 January 1826. [NRS.S/H]

LEGGAT, WALTER, born 1785 in Hawick, Roxburghshire, a merchant in New York by 1827, died there on 30 September 1850. [ANY]

LEIGHTON, WILLIAM, son of John Leighton a schoolmaster in Temple, Mid Lothian, was apprenticed to John Steel a saddle and beltmaker in Edinburgh on 10 November 1796. [ERA]

LEITCH, GEORGE, in Darnick Vale near Melrose, Roxburghshire, a mutual disposition with his wife Mary Moss, 1842. [NRS.S/H]

LENNOX, ARCHIBALD, son of Colin Lennox a gardener in Broughton, was apprenticed to Patrick Fairlie a weaver on 12 August 1790. [ERA]

LILLIE, JOHN, a lime burner in Fort Wayne, Indiana, son and heir of John Lillie, a feuar in Greenlaw, Berwickshire, who died on 1 April 1858. [NRS.S/H]

LILLIE, JOHN, born 18 December 1812 in Kelso, Roxburghshire, was educated at Edinburgh University in 1833, a minister and schoolmaster in New York, died in Kingston, N.Y. on 23 February 1867. [ANY]

LILLIE, WILLIAM, born 4 February 1802 in Kelso, Roxburghshire, emigrated to New York in1835, a leather merchant there, died in Edinburgh on 16 January 1863. [ANY]

LINDORS, JAMES, born 1821, died at Phantassie on 29 July 1896, husband of Janet Torr, born 1806, died on 20 September1874. [Innerwick gravestone, East Lothian]

LINDSAY, ALEXANDER, MD, of Pinkieburn, Musselburgh, was admitted as a burgess and guilds-brother of Ayr on 18 September 1800. [ABR]

LISTON, ROBERT RAMAGE, from Maryland, died in New Garden, Queensferry, on 6 January 1825, husband of Janet, testament, 1825. [NRS.CC8.8.150]

LISTON, THOMAS, Paymaster of the Royal Linlithgow Volunteers, was admitted as a burgess and guilds-brother of Dunfermline, Fife, on 15 August 1804. [DM]

LOCKIE, JAMES, a merchant in Dunbar, East Lothian, in 1830. [NRS.SC40.20.154.10]

LOGAN, GEORGE, born 1776, died 1 June 1853, husband of Janet Walker, born 1792, died 4 May 1839. [Eccles gravestone, Berwickshire]

LINDSAY, JAMES, of Gualaaguayehu, son of William Lindsay in Stanhope, Peebles-shire, died at the residence of R. Runciman in Buenos Ayres, Argentina, on 24 April 1877, testament, 1878, [NRS.SC70.1.189/185] [S.10563]

LOGAN, JAMES, born 1816, son of John Logan and his wife Agnes Thomson, settled in New Zealand, died in Eccles, Berwickshire, on 22 August 1893. [Eccles gravestone]

LOGAN, MARGARET, daughter of Lieutenant Colonel Logan, married J. S. Mack of the Sheriff's Office in Edinburgh, at Ferney Castle, Ayton, Berwickshire, on 11 October 1822. [SM.90.631]

LOGAN, PATRICK, born 1795, son of Abraham Logan of Burnhouses, Captain of the 57th Regiment of Foot, who died in Australia in 1834. [Lamberton gravestone, Berwickshire]

LOVELL, JOHN, in Lee, North America, brother and heir of James Lovell, a papermaker in Penicuik, Mid Lothian, who died on 16 February 1848. [NRS.S/H]

LOW, ELIZA CARTWRIGHT, youngest daughter of William Low in Portobello, Mid Lothian, wife of Reverend Augustus Sullivan minister in San Salvador, in the Bahamas, died in Arthur Town, Bahamas, on 9 December 1866. [S.7312]

LUGTON, GEORGE, born 1798, son of William Lugton and his wife Catherne Hood, died in Kyneton, Victoria, Australia, on 16 October 1869. [Ayton gravestone, Berwickshire]

LUNDIE, GEORGE ARCHIBALD, born 31 December 1819 in Kelso, Roxburghshire, son of Reverend Robert Lundie and his wife Mary Gray, a missionary in Samoa who died 'amid the converted heathen at the mission station at Leone Bay, Tutuila, in the South Seas' in September 1841. [F.2.73] [Kelso gravestone]

LYELL, GEORGE, in Portobello, Mid Lothian, died 10 May 1832, father of George Simpson Lyell in New South Wales, Australia. [NRS.S/H]

LYALL, ROBERT, in Green Mains, Auchincraw, testament, 1791, Comm. Lauder. [NRS]

LYALL, ROBERT, in Eyemouth, Berwickshire, a summons in 1831. [NRS.267.27.258.4207]

MACK, ALEXANDER, born in East Fortune in 1789, died in Kraggakama on 4 September 1876. [Port Elizabeth gravestone, South Africa]

MCARA, ARCHIBALD, born 1804, son of James McAra [1768-1810], and his wife Isabella Douglas [1778-1852], died in Valparaiso, Chile, on 19 June 1846. [Cramond gravestone, Mid Lothian]

MCARTHUR, JEAN, a brewer in South Queensferry, West Lothian, versus Allan Grant a writer in Canongate, Edinburgh, a Process of Divorce in 1808. [NRS.CC8.6.1321]

MCBRAIRE, JOHN JOSEPH, son of James MacBraire of Tweed Hill, Berwick-on-Tweed, formerly in St John's, Newfoundland, married a daughter of B. Gott of Leeds, Yorkshire, there in August 1831. [RGNA.25.10.1831]

MACCREA, JULIA, in Portobello, Midlothian, a letter in 1838. [NRS.GD113.5.499.52]

MCCRIE, JOHN, a writer in Dunbar, East Lothian, a Process of Divorce against his spouse Marion Welsh in 1806. [NRS.CC8.6.1280]

MCCULLOCH, JAMES, born 1808 in Peebles, a labourer in Marfield Powder Mill, Penicuik, Midlothian, was accused of discharging a firearm and wounding in 1832. [NRS.AD14.32.384]

MCDOUGALL, ELIZABETH, born 1800, daughter of John McDougall, [1771-1849], tenant in Foulden, died at Three Rivers, Lower Canada, on 22 November 1850. [Foulden gravestone, Berwickshire]

MCDOUGAL, JAMES, born 1737, a farmer, died at Whitfield, Peeblesshire, on 17 September 1822. [SM.22.632]

MCDOUGALL, THOMAS, a butcher in Kingston, Canada, grandson and heir of William McDougall, a weaver in Kelso, Roxburghshire, who died on 6 January 1851. [NRS.S/H]

MCDOUGALL, WILLIAM, late of Tobago, youngest son of Reverend Dr McDougall in Makerstoun, Roxburghshire, died in Antigua on 11 February 1825. [AJ.4033]

MACFARLANE, JAMES, an Excise supervisor in Dunbar, East Lothian, a process of scandal and defamation, 1795. [NRS.CC8.6.960]

MCGAVIN, CATHERINE, wife of Thomas Fairley in Broxburn, West Lothian, was accused of murdering their daughter Mary Fairley in 1846. [AD14.46.296]

MCGIBBON, ALEXANDER, of Crawhill, town-clerk of Queensferry, West Lothian, father of David McGibbon who died in Montreal, Quebec, on 2 August 1827. [BM.21119]

MCGRAINGER, J. agent for the British Linen Company in Kelso, Roxburghshire, in 1849. [POD]

MCGUIRE, PETER, born 1791 in Ireland, a strapper and horse-keeper in Haddington, East Lothian, was accused of mobbing and rioting there in 1831. [NRS.AD14.3358]

MCINTOSH, ROBERT, a merchant in Eyemouth, Berwickshire, testament, 1798, Comm. Lauder. [NRS]

MCKAY, AGNES, in Townhead, Jedburgh, Roxburghshire, a victim of reckless driving in 1829. [NRS.AD14.29.216]

MCKAY, ANGUS, born 1794, son of John McKay, died at the Battle of Waterloo on 18 June 1815. [Eccles gravestone, Berwickshire]

MCKECHNIE, Reverend W., a minister in Musselburgh, Mid Lothian, father of James, born 1796, a surgeon who died in Hanover, Jamaica, on 10 January 1818. [DPCA.815]

MCKENZIE, ALEXANDER, in Port Seton, East Lothian, in 1792. [NRS.JP2.6.3.4.8]

MCKENZIE, JAMES, born 1803 in Roxburghshire, a plasterer from Greenock then in Charleston, was admitted as a citizen of South Carolina on 5 August 1823. [NARA.M1183.1]

MCKENZIE, JOHN, a skipper in North Berwick, East Lothian, dead by 1818. [NRS.S/H]

MCKENZIE, WILLIAM, in West Linton, Peebles-shire, applied to settle in Canada on 7 March 1815. [NRS.RH9]

MACKINLAY, WILLIAM, in Canada West, son and heir of Matthew MacKinlay, a collier in Tranent, East Lothian, in 1859. [NRS.S/H]

MACKNIGHT, WILLIAM, MD, born 22 April 1771, son of Reverend Thomas Somerville and his wife Martha Chalmers in Jedburgh, Roxburghshire, died in Florence, Italy, on 26 June 1860. [F.2.128]

MCLAGAN, HECTOR, born 26 June 1768 in Melrose, Roxburghshire, son of Reverend Frederick McLagan and his wife Christian Turnbull, died in Jamaica on 11 September 1908. [F.2.188]

MCLEAN, MURDOCH, a Lieutenant of the 42nd Regiment, was admitted as a burgess of Musselburgh, Mid Lothian, on 2 February 1811. [NRS.GD174.2405.12]

MCLEAN, NORMAN, born 1813, son of Charles McLean in Gavinton, died in New York on 12 February 1851. [Langton gravestone, Berwickshire]

MCLEOD, JOHN, in Tyningham, East Lothian, father of Christian McLeod who married James B. MacKinlay, a broker and commission agent in Buenos Ayres, Argentina, in Salta, Argentina, on 3 September 1872. [S.9149]

MACRAE, ALEXANDER ARCHIBALD, son of Alexander MacRae in Demerara, died in Portobello, Mid Lothian, on 10 July 1854. [EEC.22605]

MCWATT, DAVID, messenger at arms in Duns, Berwickshire, 1849. [POD]

MCWHIRTER, J. A., agent for the Western Bank of Scotland in Portobello, Mid Lothian, in 1849. [POD]

MABON, ALEXANDER, [1824-1890], and his wife Jane Barns, parents of Adam Mabon, born 1856. [Whitsome gravestone, Berwickshire]

MACK, ALEXANDER, born 1789 in East Fortune, East Lothian, died in Kraggakama, South Africa, on 4 September 1876. [St George gravestone, Port Elizabeth, Cape of Good Hope]

MACK, JOSEPH GARDNER, born 1806, died in Berrybank, Victoria, Australia, on 21 July 1868. [Coldingham gravestone, Berwickshire]

MACK, THOMAS, in Kingston, Jamaica from 1786 until 1795, thereafter a tenant in Gordon Mains, Berwickshire, 1800. [NRS.CS26.912.14]

MAIR, THOMAS, a blacksmith in Broxburn, West Lothian, applied to settle in Canada on 3 March 1815. [NRS.RH9]

MANN, Reverend JAMES, born 1801, son of John Mann and his wife Isabel Hart, in Duns, Berwickshire, died in Falmouth, Jamaica, on 10 February 1830. [Duns gravestone]

MANUEL, JOHN, a brewer in Stobs by Dalkeith, Mid Lothian, 1823. [NRS.CS271.47]

MARSHALL, WALTER, son of Robert Marshall a surgeon in Peebles, was apprenticed to Walter Brunton, a saddler and beltmaker in Edinburgh, for six years on 31 January 1799. [ERA]

MARTIN, JOHN, son of David Martin a brewer in Musselburgh, Mid Lothian, was apprenticed to Robert Gourlay a haberdasher in Edinburgh on 9 February 1792. [ERA]

MARTIN, MATTHEW, born 1801 in Kelso, Roxburghshire, was accused of jail-breaking in 1816. [NRS.AD14.16.16]

MARTIN, ROBERT, son of Reverend Samuel Martin and his wife Jessie Weir, was drowned in the St John River, South Africa, on 12 January 1842. [Kirkton gravestone, Bathgate, West Lothian]

MASON, EUPHEMIA, born 1833, wife of Robert Spark, died in Melbourne, Australia, on 26 November 1890. [Westruther gravestone, Berwickshire]

MASON, JOHN, born 1787, a distiller in Kelso, Roxburghshire, died on 26 May 1844. [Kelso gravestone]

MASON, ROBERT, born 1774, a watchmaker in Kelso, Roxburghshire, died on 20 May 1831, husband of Christian Wilson, born 1778, died on 6 November 1849. [Kelso gravestone]

MASON, ROBERT, in Rockford, Illinois, son and heir of Robert Mason, a shoemaker in South Queensferry, West Lothian, who died on 17 March 1853. [NRS.S/H]

MASON, WILLIAM, a sailor in Grangepans, West Lothian, was accused of poaching in 1825. [NRS.B48.16.6.6]

MASTERTON, WILLIAM, in Bathgate, West Lothian, was found guilty of poaching in 1825. [NRS.B48.16.6.6]

MATHESON, PETER, born on 13 March 1838, in Selkirk, a missionary in Madras, India, from 1876 until his death on 20 January 1877. [F.7.701]

MATHIESON, WILLIAM, a weaver in Earlston, Roxburghshire, son and heir of John Mathieson a portioner of Gattonside, 1844. [NRS.S/H]

MAXWELL, JOHN, second son of William Maxwell in Carriden, West Lothian, died in Tobago on 22 October 1793. [SM][EA] [GM.63.1214]

MAXWELL, JOHN STRANGE, in Toronto, Ontario, cousin and heir of James Warrach, a brewer in Anderston, Glasgow, later in Prestonpans, East Lothian, who died on 27 January 1814. [NRS.S/H]

MAXWELL, JOHN, in New York, brother and heir of William Maxwell in West Nisbet, Berwickshire, in 1842. [NRS.S/H]

MEEK, ROBERT, born 1786 in East Lothian, died in St John, New Brunswick, on 5 March 1825. [New Brunswick Courier, 5.3.1825]

MEIKLE, JOHN, was accused of culpable and furious driving a cart in Currie, Mid Lothian, in 1825. [NRS.AD14.25.36]

MEIKLE, WILLIAM, a fisherman in Queensferry, West Lothian, subscribed to a bond of caution for John Ferguson and Thomas Henderson, fishermen in Queensferry in 1803. [NRS.CS271.746]

MEIKLEJOHN, JOHN, of Eyemouth, Berwickshire, was admitted as a burgess and guilds-brother of Dunfermline, Fife, on 16 June 1796. [DM]

MEIN, JAMES, late from Jamaica, now in Newstead, Roxburghshire, a sasine, 1820. [NRS.RS.Roxburgh.5629]

MELDRUM, Miss, married James Oliver from Georgia, in Berwick-on-Tweed, Northumberland, in November 1804. [SM.66.971]

MELROSE, ROBERT, in St John, New Brunswick, son and heir of Robert Melrose, a dairyman in Galashiels, Selkirkshire, who died on 12 December 1868. [NRS.S/H]

MENZIES, JOHN MCNAUGHTON, youngest son of John Menzies of Culdares, residing in Penicuik, Mid Lothian, versus his wife Euphemia Christie in the Canongate, Edinburgh, a Process of Adherence in 1823. [NRS.CC8.6.1879]

MERCER, ISABELLA, wife of George Rutherford of Sunnyside, only child of Andrew Mercer of Lochbreast, Roxburghshire, heir to her grandfather John Mercer of Lochbreast, 1847. [NRS.S/H]

MERCER, JOHN, in Woolwich, England, a Sergeant of the Royal Artillery, heir to his father John Mercer, a weaver and portioner in Bridgend, Roxburghshire, 4 April 1793. [NRS.S/H]

MEUROS, GEORGE, son of Thomas Meuros a mealmaker in Dalkeith, Mid Lothian, was apprenticed to James Duguid a merchant in Edinburgh on 28 April 1796. [ERA]

MICHIE, RACHEL, daughter of James Michie once a slater now a grocer in Kelso, Roxburghshire, and his wife Elizabeth Scott now wife of William Jeffrey Aimers in Kelso, heir to her maternal grand-father James Scott a wright in Kelso, 1845. [NRS.S/H]

MICKLE, ALEXANDER, born 1829, son of David Mickle and his wife Isabella Lilly, died on 24 November 1861, buried in Cranbourne, Melbourne, Victoria, Australia. [Duns, Berwickshire, gravestone]

MIDDLEMISS, GEORGE, in Bellville, born 1728, died 17 November 1810, husband of Margaret Currie, born 1743, died 10 February 1800. [Eccles gravestone, Berwickshire]

MIDDLEMAS, JOSEPH, from Yetholm, Roxburghshire, a divinity student in 1825, later a minister in Bethlehem, Albany County, New York. [AUPC]

MILLER, ADAM, born 1790 in Roxburghshire, died in Halifax, Nova Scotia, on 26 March 1833. [HJ.1.4.1833]

MILLER, THOMAS, a fisherman in Fisher Row, Mid Lothian, testament, 1803, Comm. Edinburgh. [NRS]

MILLER, THOMAS, born 1728, formerly in New York, died in North Berwick, East Lothian, on 15 July 1814. [GM.84.190]

MILLER, THOMAS, born 1821, son of James Miller, died in Napier, Hawke's Bay, New Zealand, on 30 May 1863. [Chirnside gravestone, Berwickshire]

MILLIGAN, DAVID, son of Robert Milligan of Roslin, Mid Lothian, died in Spanish Town, Jamaica, in 1818. [BM.3.248]

MILLIKEN, MARGARET Q., daughter of William Milliken in St Vincent, died at Brunstane House, Portobello, Mid Lothian, on 24 May 1823. [SM.91.776]

MILNE, DAVID, factor of Billie Estate, Berwickshire, letters, from 1833 to 1846. [NRS.GD267.25.69]

MILNE, NICOL, son and heir of Nicol Milne of Faldonside, Roxburghshire, 1841. [NRS.S/H]

MILNE, NICOL, of Whitehill, only son of James Milne of Whitehill, nephew and heir of Thomas Milne farmer at Newark, Roxburghshire, 1841. [NRS.S/H]

MILROY, DAVID, born 16 December 1831 in Crailing, Roxburghshire, son of Reverend Andrew Milroy and his wife Margaret Bryce, a physician surgeon who died in Bermuda on 3 September 1864. [F.2.109]

MINTO, WALTER, born 5 December 1753 in Coldingham, Berwickshire, emigrated to America in 1786, Professor of Mathematics at the College of New Jersey in 1787, died in Princeton, N.J. on 21 October 1796. [WA][UPC]

MITCHELL, DAVID, in Canada, son and heir of Elizabeth Anderson, wife of Andrew Anderson, a manufacturer in Livingstone, West Lothian, in 1802. [NRS.S/H]

MITCHELL, GEORGE, son of James Mitchell a farmer at Tabroun, East Lothian, was apprenticed to Robert Brown a baker in Edinburgh on 23 May 1793. [ERA]

MITCHELL, JAMES, a shipmaster in Bo'ness, West Lothian, 1800. [NRS.S/H]

MITCHELL, MARGARET ELIZABETH, daughter of Alexander Mitchell of Gargrogo, at Troqueer Holm, Peebles-shire, on 15 September 1813. [SM.75.799]

MITCHELL, SARAH, in Jedburgh, Roxburghshire, relict of George Selkirk a wright there, and Margaret Mitchell, heirs to their sister Elizabeth Mitchell in Jedburgh, relict of Daniel Fraser a merchant tailor in Quebec, 1826. [NRS.S/H]

MITCHELL, T., master of the John of Bo'ness trading between Leith and Quebec in 1817. [NRS.E504.22.7]

MITCHELL, WILLIAM, born 1838, son of John Mitchell in Yair, Selkirkshire, died in Melbourne, Australia, on 27 December 1898. [S.17352]

MOFFAT, ADAM P., born 1841, from Mount Pleasant, Berwickshire, died in Cardoba on 11 April 1875. [EC.28292]

MOFFAT, ALEXANDER, born 1803, son of Andrew Moffat, [1768-1845], a baker in Duns, Berwickshire, died in Charleston, South Carolina, on 17 September 1819. [Duns gravestone]

MOFFAT, ANDREW, born 1794, son of Andrew Moffat, [1768-1845], a baker in Duns, Berwickshire, a merchant in Charleston, South Carolina, was admitted as citizen of S.C. on 14 February 1820, died on Sullivan's Island, S.C., on 22 August 1849. [NARA.M1183.1] [Duns gravestone]

MOFFAT, ANDREW, born 1820, son of John Moffat, [1791-1857], died in America on 26 June 1860. [Kelso gravestone, Roxburghshire]

MOFFAT, DAVID, born 1810 in Musselburgh, Mid Lothian, a currier who settled in New York in 1827, died at Cold Spring on the Hudson River, on 24 July 1887. [ANY]

MOFFATT, GEORGE, born 1800, son of Andrew Moffat, [1768-1845], a baker in Duns, Berwickshire, died in Charleston, South Carolina, died on 21 August 1844. [Duns gravestone]

MOFFAT, ISABELLA, wife of Thomas Polwarth, a butcher in Leitholm, Berwickshire, daughter and heir of Margaret Dods, wife of Robert Dods in Canada, in 1870. [NRS.S/H]

MOFFAT, JAMES, son of David Moffat a tanner in Musselburgh, Mid Lothian, husband of Jean Hogg, settled in Quebec before 1816. [NRS.GD81.310.1]

MOFFAT, THOMAS, son of Thomas Moffat a tanner in Musselburgh, Mid Lothian, died in Glasgow, Montana, on 21 July 1846. [EEC.21413]

MOIR, PETER, a surgeon in East Linton, Berwickshire, papers, 1835. [NRS.GD267.24.2]

MOODIE, Lady ANNE, in Georgia, heir to her grandfather John McKenzie, a skipper in North Berwick, East Lothian, in 1818. [NRS.S/H]

MOODIE, MARGARET, widow of John Affleck, a farmer in Columbus, Ohio, daughter and heir of James Moodie, portioner of Nungate, Haddington, East Lothian, who died on 5 March 1827. [NRS.S/H]

MORISON, JAMES, an innkeeper in Dalkeith, Midlothia, property writs, 1820-1824. [NRS.GD224.952.84]

MORRISON, JOHN, born 1795, second son of James Morrison of the White Hart Inn in Dalkeith, Mid Lothian, a surgeon who died in Kingston, Jamaica, on 6 August 1819. [S.3.144.19] [EA]

MORTON, AGNES, daughter of .... Morton and his wife Elisabeth Aitchison, [1757-1832], settled in Upper Canada. [Birgham gravestone, Berwickshire]

MOW, JOHN, of Mains, Chirnside, Berwickshire, testament, 1795, Comm. Lauder. [NRS]

MOWAT, WILLIAM, son of James Mowat a weaver in Wrighthouses, was apprenticed to William Begbie a tailor in Edinburgh, for six years, in 1797. [ERA]

MUIR, JAMES, born 1815 in Peebles, died on 26 June 1838. [Second Presbyterian gravestone, Charleston, South Carolina]

MUIR, JOHN, born 21 April 1838 in Dunbar, East Lothian, son of Daniel Muir and Ann Gilroy, a naturalist, died in Los Angeles, California on 24 December 1914.

MUIR, THOMAS, in Alexandria, Virginia, son and heir of John Muir, a portioner of Newstead, Roxburghshire, in 1802. [NRS.S/H]

MUIRHEAD, JAMES, a shipmaster in Dunbar, East Lothian, testament, 1811, Comm. Edinburgh. [NRS]

MURDOCH, WILLIAM, in Halifax, Nova Scotia, heir of Agnes Cuming in Hawick, Roxburghshire, in 1852. [NRS.S/H]

MURRAY, ALEXANDER MCGRIGOR, from Joppa, Mid Lothian, in Little Gunpowder, Harford County, Maryland, a sasine, 1852. [NRS.RS. Glasgow.1455]

MURRAY, ANDREW, born 11 May 1839 in Melrose, Roxburghshire, son of Reverend William Murray and his wife Agnes Cunningham, died in Burwood, New South Wales, Australia, on 8 February 1895. [F.2.189]

MURRAY, CHARLES, son of John Murray of Philiphaugh, Roxburghshire, settled at Quinta do Bello Monte, Funchal, the British Consul in Madeira, died in Lisbon, Portugal, in March 1808. [ARM] [SM.70.398] [OW.36]; his wife, daughter of Robert Scott of Crailing, Roxburghshire, died in Edinburgh on 1 December 1806. [SM.69.78]

MURRAY, DAVID, son of John Murray a schoolmaster in Musselburgh, Mid Lothian, was apprenticed to George Leslie and William Scott, insurance brokers in Edinburgh, for five years in 1798. [ERA]

MURRAY, DAVID, son of John Murray a farmer in Lasswade, Midlothian, was apprenticed to George Rae a candlemaker in Edinburgh, for five years, in 1799. [ERA]

MURRAY, GEORGE, minister at North Berwick, East Lothian, died on 17 August 1822. [SM.90.520]

MURRAY, JAMES, a kitchen gardener in Dunbar, East Lothian, financial accounts from 1808 to 1822. [NRS.CS96.2651.2]

MURRAY, WILLIAM, born 1842, son of James Murray in Slatehouse, Jedburgh, Roxburghshire, died in Callao, Peru, on 18 March 1868. [S.7724]

MUSCHET, Dr GEORGE, in British Guina, youngest son of Richard Muschet a merchant in Dalkeith, Mid Lothian, died in St Kitts on 24 March 1860. [S.1517]

MUSHET, WILLIAM, in Dalkeith, Mid Lothian, father of John MacFarlane Mushet who died in Lexington, Kentucky, on 1 December 1884. [S.12919]

NAPIER, ALEXANDER, Captain of the Royal Linlithgow Volunteers, was admitted as a burgess and guilds-brother of Dunfermline in 1804. [DM]

NAPIER, CHRISTOPHER, a physician and surgeon in Grenada, son of Christopher Napier an Excise officer in Prestonpans, East Lothian, a deed, 1790. [NRS.RD2.250.599]

NASMYTH, Sir JAMES, died in 1829, husband of Eleanora Murray who died in 1807, daughter of John Murray of Philiphaugh. [Dawyck gravestone, Peebles-shire]

NEIL, GEORGE, a stationer in Haddington, East Lothian, versus Barbara Lutit and their children Neil and David, in the Canongate, Edinburgh, a Process of Declarator of Marriage in 1810. [NRS.CC8.6.1387]

NEILSON, ALEXANDER, born 1791 in Atholstaneford, East Lothian, a mason in Garleton, Haddington, was accused of mobbing and rioting there in 1831. [NRS.AD14.3358]

NEILSON, JAMES, from Haddington, East Lothian, a member of the Scots Charitable Society of Boston in 1817. [SCS/NEHGS]

NESBIT, ROBERT, born on 17 November 1799 in Berwick-on-Tweed, settled in Waccamaw, South Carolina in 1808, a planter who was naturalised in Charleston, S.C., on 30 March 1825, died on 17 October 1848. [Waccamaw gravestone] [NARA.M1183.1]

NEWALL, ROBERT, a farmer from Hawick, Roxburghshire, with Sarah his wife, and two children, emigrated via Greenock to Canada in 1815. [TNA.CO385.2]

NEWLANDS, JAMES, son of William Newlands in Portobello, Mid Lothian, was apprenticed to John Spottiswood a merchant and ironmonger in Edinburgh on 21 October 1799. [ERA]

NEWLANDS, JOHN, born 1792, a smith in Nungate, Haddington, East Lothian, died on 31 January 1841, husband of Margaret Dods, born 1790, died 5 November 1870. [Morham gravestone, East Lothian]

NEWTON, FRANCIS, born 1713, son of Reverend Newton in Earlston, Berwickshire, a Jacobite in 1745, a merchant in Funchal, Madeira, in 1754, died in London after 1809. [ARM][OW]

NIBBLE, DAVID, son of Archibald Nibblie a farmer in Elphinstone, East Lothian, was apprenticed to Alexander Logan a baker in Edinburgh on 15 April 1790. [ERA]

NICHOLL, JAMES, messenger at arms, Linlithgow, West Lothian, 1849. [POD]

NICHOLSON, J. W., a farmer in Nisbet, East Lothian, father of Thomas William Nicholson, who died in Bahia Blanca, Argentina, on 7 October 1884. [S.12906]

NICHOLSON, Reverend MAXWELL, and his wife Frances Oliphant in Pencaitland, East Lothian, parents of Francis Maxwell Nicholson, born 24 December 1855, a merchant in Buenos Ayres, Argentina, and of Stuart Oliphant Nicholson, born 29 January 1849, a cotton merchant in New Orleans, Louisiana. [F.1.116]

NIMMO, AGNES, in White Banks, West Lothian, versus her husband David Reid in Linlithgow, West Lothian, a Process of Adherence in 1828, followed by a Process of Divorce in 1829. [NRS.CC8.6.2084/2145]

NISBET, CHARLES, born 21 January 1736 in Haddington, East Lothian, son of William Nisbet, was educated at Edinburgh University, a minister in Montrose, Angus, emigrated to America in 1785, President of Dickenson College, Carlyle, Pennsylvania, brother of Andrew Nisbet minister at Garvald, a deed subscribed in Cumberland County, Pa., on 5 May 1800, died on 18 January 1804. [NRS.RD3.286.415] [WA][F.5.411]

NISBET, PETER, a carter in Eyemouth, Berwickshire, a summons in 1831. [NRS.267.27.258.4207]

NISBET, ROBERT, of Mersington, born 1790, a Lieutenant Colonel and formerly Captain of the Light Dragoons, fought in the Peninsular War and at Waterloo, died on 25 July 1865, husband of Mary ...., born 1790, died 3 February 1864. [Eccles gravestone, Berwickshire]

NISBET, WILLIAM, in Duns, Berwickshire, a former Corporal of the 94th Regiment of Foot, applied to settle in Canada on 14 April 1819. [TNA.CO384.5.373]

NOBLE, AGNES, in Jamaica, a sasine, 2 December 1815. [NRS.RS.Queensferry.1.85]

NOBLE, ROBERT, son of Robert Noble, a teacher in Peebles who died in December 1793, and his wife Janet Grieve, [1750-1836], died in Halifax, Nova Scotia, in 1846. [Peebles gravestone]

O'CONNACHER, JAMES, a skipper in Bo'ness, West Lothian, testament, 1804, Comm. Edinburgh, [NRS]; his widow Helen Melly, testament, 1813, Comm. Edinburgh. [NRS]

OLIVER, ANDREW, messenger at arms, Hawick, Roxburghshire, 1849. [POD]

OLIVER, GEORGE, born 1781 at Blinkbonny, Castleton, Roxburghshire, son of William Oliver and his wife Jean Nicol, married Elizabeth Irving, settled in Indiana, died in 1837. [OS]

OLIVER, HENRY, born 1795 in Selkirkshire, died at Beaverbank, Nova Scotia, on 10 December 1832. [AR.15.12.1832]

OLIVER, JAMES, born 1774 in Berwick on Tweed, Northumberland, a planter who died in Savanna, Georgia, on 26 May 1808. [Savanna Republican, 28.5.1808]

OLIVER, ROBERT, born 1777, son of John Oliver and his wife Margaret Douglas, in Wilton, Roxburghshire, emigrated to Nova Scotia in 1814, died in 1870s. [OS]

OLIVER, THOMAS, a smith in America, son and heir of Thomas Oliver, a nailer in Denholm, Roxburghshire, in 1858. [NRS.S/H]

OLIVER, WILLIAM, born 31 January 1795 in Hawick, Roxburghshire, son of Robert Oliver, a shoemaker, and his wife Helen Scott, emigrated to America. [OS]

OLIVER, WILLIAM, a dyer in Jedburgh, Roxburghshire, later in Edinburgh, brother and heir of Mary Oliver in New York, in 1846. [NRS.S/H]

OMAN, ROBERT, son of William Oman the Rector of Peebles Grammar School, was apprenticed to Alexander Laidlaw, a white iron smith in Edinburgh, for six years, on 1 July 1790. [ERA]

OMIT, WALTER, a quarryman in Swineburn, Kirkliston, West Lothian, was accused of night poaching with an offensive weapon there, in 1830. [NRS.AD14.30.260]

ORD, EDWARD, son of Reverend Ord in Longformacus, Berwickshire, a surgeon who died in Jamaica in December 1805. [DPCA]

ORMISTON, JANE, wife of William Francis Blackhall, died in Des Moines, Iowa, on 4 March 1886. [Cockburnspath gravestone, Berwickshire]

ORMSTON, JAMES, a merchant in Kelso, Roxburghshire, eldest son of James Ormston a barber and innkeeper there, heir to his uncle Charles Ormston a skinner in Kelso, 18 August 1790. [NRS.S/H]

PALMER, JOHN, probably born in Kelso, Roxburghshire, settled as a merchant in New York in 1799, married Margaret Given, died 1 February 1858. [ANY]

PANTON, Reverend GEORGE, formerly in Shelborne, Nova Scotia, and New York, lately in Kelso, Roxburghshire, probate, October 1810, Prerogative Court of Canterbury. [TNA]

PARK, DAVID BOYD, a sailmaker in Norfolk, Virginia, son and heir of David Park in Peebles in 1837. [NRS.S/H]

PARK, THOMAS CRAIGIE, from Springfield, Haddington, East Lothian, married Maggie Tupp, daughter of Reverend Dr A. Tupp, in Knox Church, Toronto, Ontario, on 11 June 1874. [AJ.6597]

PATERSON, ARCHIBALD, a farmer in Santa Clara, California, nephew and heir of Christian Baxter in Prestonpans, East Lothian, who died on 6 May

1860, also, heir to his aunt Janet Baxter, wife of Peter Brown, a farmer in Broadoak, Shropshire, England, who died on 9 April 1843. [NRS.S/H]

PATERSON, ELIZABETH, born 1780, daughter of John Paterson, [1747-1831], and his wife Jean Tweedie, [1742-1821], died in Long Grove, Iowa, on 2 December 1866. [West Linton gravestone, Peebles-shire]

PATTERSON, ISABELLA, born 1818, daughter of George Paterson and his wife Mary Douglas, wife of William Sherlaw, died in New Zealand on 14 February 1871. [Ayton gravestone, Berwickshire]

PATERSON, J., messenger at arms, Selkirk, 1849. [POD]

PATERSON, J., agent for the Edinburgh and Glasgow Bank in Penicuik, Midlothian, in 1849. [POD]

PATERSON, JOHN, a weaver in Belhaven, East Lothian, was accused of rioting in Dunbar in 1816. [NRS.SC40.54.1.31]

PATERSON, NEIL WILLIAM, born 1779, son of John Paterson, [1747-1831], and his wife Jean Tweedie, [1742-1821], died in Montreal, Quebec, on 21 July 1834. [West Linton gravestone, Peebles-shire]

PATERSON, ROBERT, a merchant in Quebec, married Grace Denholm, eldest daughter of H. Denholm of Birthwood, there on 11 March 1822. [S.271.102]

PATERSON, WILLIAM, born 1771, a carter in Allanton, Edrom, Berwickshire, accused of the murder of William Mack in Eyemouth, Berwickshire, 1833. [NRS.AD14.33.379]

PATERSON, Reverend WILLIAM, and his wife Jessie Hay Spence, in Cockburnspath, Berwickshire, parents of William Gilbert Spence Paterson, born 30 August 1854, later the British Consul in Reykyavik, Iceland, who died on 28 March 1898. [F.1.405]

PATON, EDWARD, born 5 December 1834 in Ancrum, Roxburghshire, son of Reverend John Paton and his wife Mary, a merchant in Pernambuco, Brazil. [F.2.101]; he married Mary Gibson, eldest daughter of Henry Gibson in Pernambuco, there on 22 April 1869. [S.8054]

PATON, JAMES, born 13 September 1798, son of Reverend John Paton and his wife Margaret Main in Lasswade, Mid Lothian, a Captain of the Bengal Artillery, in India, died in 1848. [F.I.330]

PATON, JAMES, born 1 June 1839 in Ancrum, Roxburghshire, son of Reverend John Paton and his wife Mary, settled in Canada. [F.2.101]

PATON, JOHN, born 26 May 1831 in Ancrum, Roxburghshire, son of Reverend John Paton and his wife Mary, a banker in New York, died 30 March 1908. [F.2.101]

PATON, THOMAS, born in April 1806, son of Reverend John Paton and his wife Margaret Main in Lasswade, Mid Lothian, a banker in Canada and in New Zealand. [F.1.330]

PATON, THOMAS, a banker in Canada, brother and heir of Peter Paton, in Lasswade, Midlothian, who died on 8 October 1857. [NRS.S/H]

PAUL, ARCHIBALD, son of Andrew Paul in Linlithgow, West Lothian, died in St Ann's, Jamaica, on 30 September 1822. [EEC.17375]

PAUL, GEORGE, born 1827, a master mariner, died in Karachi, East India, on 30 March 1869, husband of Elizabeth Thompson, born 1836, died in Kelso, Roxburghshire, on 28 March 1868. [Kelso gravestone]

PEACOCK, AGNES, in Tranent, East Lothian, versus her spouse Alexander Teviotdale a plasterer in Edinburgh, a Process of Divorce in 1807. [NRS.CC8.6.1289]

PEARSON, ADAM, born 1817 in Cockenzie, East Lothian, son of Adam Pearson and his wife Jane Stewart, a merchant in New York who died in Edinburgh on 29 July 1889. [ANY]

PEARSON, DAVID, born 10 December 1821 in Cockenzie, East Lothian, son of Adam Pearson and his wife Jane Stewart, a book-keeper in New York who died on 18 March 1886. [ANY]

PENMAN, DANIEL, son of David Penman an innkeeper in Duddingston, Mid Lothian, was apprenticed to James Donald a druggist in Edinburgh in May 1797. [ERA]

PETTIGREW, ROBERT, born in 1783 in East Lothian, a labourer, with his wife Eleanor, born 1782 in East Lothian, and family, John born 1805, Margaret born 1807, Jane born 1808, Ellen born 1812, and Ann born 1815, emigrated via Leith to America, and were naturalised in New York on 1 November 1826. [NARA]

PHILIPS, GEORGE, in Jamaica, son and heir of William Philips, a mason in Hawick, Roxburghshire, in 1809. [NRS.SH]

PHILIPS, THOMAS, a skipper in Dunbar, East Lothian, testament, 1826, Comm. Edinburgh. [NRS]

PIRIE, JOHN, a surgeon major, died in Bombay, India, on 18 January 1870. [Kelso gravestone, Roxburghshire]

PITTILLO, JOHN, born 1784, a horse dealer, died on 18 April 1861, husband of Mary Purves, born 1792, died 25 August 1870. [Kelso gravestone, Roxburghshire]

PLENDERLEITH, JAMES, born 1793, a farmer at Nether Horsburgh, died on 4 June 1878, husband of Margaret Lawson, born in 1785, died on 2 March 1878. [Eddleston gravestone, Peebles-shire]

PLENDERLEITH, ROBERT JOHN, born 1848, died in Nowgong, India, on 16 June 1877. [Eddleston gravestone, Peebles-shire]

POLWARTH, ALEXANDER, born 1806, died in Leitholm on 8 June 1870, husband of Margaret Scott, born 1805, died 28 October 1890. [Eccles gravestone, Berwickshire]

PORTEOUS, GEORGE, a currier from Haddington, East Lothian, married Frances McDonald, daughter of Alexander McDonald, in Kingston, Jamaica, on 8 July 1842. [EEC.20500]

PORTEOUS, SAMUEL, in Whitton, Jedburgh, Roxburghshire, applied to settle in Canada on 20 March 1819. [TNA.CO384.5.465]

PORTER, WILLIAM, in Virginia, heir to his cousin Ann Finlay, daughter of James Finlay of Wallyford, East Lothian, who died in November 1809. [NRS.S/H]

PRATT, WILLIAM, an innkeeper in Dunbar, East Lothian, a process of scandal and defamation, 1795. [NRS.CC8.6.960]

PRIMROSE, JOHN, Deputy Treasury Officer, son of Reverend Dr Primrose in Prestonpans, East Lothian, married Elizabeth Arrindell, daughter of Isaac Arrindell of Bequid, in Antigua on 2 May 1829, died in Kingston, St Vincent, on 19 September 1831. [BM.26.267] [AJ.4388]

PRIMROSE, NICOL, youngest son of Robert Primrose a surgeon in Musselburgh, Mid Lothian, a merchant in Charleston, South Carolina, from 1780, naturalised there on 27 February 1783, died in Charleston, S.C., on 13 November 1796. [EEC.12303] [SCSA] [CM.11785]

PRIMROSE, ROBERT, only son of Nicol Primrose in Charleston, South Carolina, grandson of Robert Primrose a surgeon in Musselburgh, Mid Lothian, died in Charleston in 1824, probate August 1825, PCC, [TNA]. [BM.15.494]

PRINGLE, ADAM, a clockmaker in Edinburgh, heir to his brother Andrew Pringle a wright in Mellerstain, Roxburghshire, 29 June 1790. [NRS.S/H]

PRINGLE, AGNES, relict of Thomas Hay, a surgeon in Kelso, Roxburghshire, now spouse of John Hermiston, a horse dealer in Kelso, a Process of Declerator of Marriage in 1817. [NRS.CC8.6.1669]

PRINGLE, AGNES, in Greenock, Renfrewshire, daughter and heir of David Pringle in Smailholm, Roxburghshire, 1845. [NRS.S/H]

PRINGLE, ANDREW, son of Dunbar Pringle a tanner, was apprenticed to Thomas Reid, a clock and watchmaker in Edinburgh, for seven years on 17 January 1793. [ERA]

PRINGLE, ANDREW, born 1779, formerly a tanner and wool merchant in Haddington, East Lothian, died at Ben Lomond, Prince William County, Virginia, on 25 January 1863. [S.2402]

PRINGLE, DAVID, born 1797, a shipwright from Dunbar, East Lothian, was drowned in the Falls, New Brunswick, on 17 November 1820. [City Gazette, 22.11.1820]

PRINGLE, JAMES, in Canada, nephew and heir of Margaret Monilaws, wife of J. Hood, a tenant farmer in Long Yester, East Lothian, in 1843. [NRS.S/H]

PRINGLE, MARK, son of John Pringle of Crichton, Mid Lothian, heir to his cousin Robert Pringle of Clifton, 22 January 1793. [NRS.S/H]

PRINGLE, ROBERT, born 1837, son of James Pringle and his wife Mary Downie, died in the Ottow River, Otago, New Zealand, on 14 February 1862. [Edrom gravestone, Berwickshire]

PRINGLE, WILLIAM, and his wife Christine Hunter, parents of Christina Pringle who died in New South Wales, Australia, on 16 February 1889. [Greenlaw gravestone, Berwickshire]

PROFIT, ALEXANDER, Deacon of the Incorporation of Shoemakers of Haddington, East Lothian, versus David Beal a shoemaker in Haddington, in 1806. [NRS.CS271/55924]

PUNTON, JAMES, [1838-1906], husband of Elizabeth Christie, [1836-1910], parents of Jane Black Punton who died in Louisiana. [Dirleton gravestone, East Lothian]

PURDIE, SAMUEL, born 1770, a wright, his wife Isobel McKechnie born 1783, from West Calder, Mid Lothian, emigrated via Greenock to Upper Canada in July 1815. [TNA.AO3; CO385.2]

PURVES, JANET, born 1812, wife of George Smith, died 29 July 1898, was buried in Booranda Cemetery, Melbourne, Australia. [Coldstream gravestone, Berwickshire]

PURVIS of PURVIS, JOHN HOME, born 1785, second son of Sir Alexander Purvis, HM Consul for Florida died in Pensacola on 30 September 1827. [BM.23.270]

PURVIS, JOHN, a feuar in Eyemouth, Berwickshire, a decreet in 1831. [NRS.267.27.260.4208]

PURVES, PATRICK, a merchant in Eyemouth, Berwickshire, testament, 1797, Comm. Lauder. [NRS]

PURVES, ROBERT KER, a seaman in Philadelphia, Pennsylvania, son and heir of Alexander Purves, a shoemaker in Dunbar, East Lothian, who died on 13 December 1861. [NRS.S/H]

PURVES, PATRICK, a merchant in Eyemouth, Berwickshire, testament, 1797, Comm. Lauder. [NRS]

PURVES, THOMAS, in Eyemouth, Berwickshire, a decreet in 1831. [NRS. GD267.27.260.4208]

PURVES, WILLIAM, farmer at Burnfoot, Roxburghshire, brother and heir of Andrew Purves in Bunhill Row, London,1843. [NRS.S/H]

PYLE, JAMES, son of James Pyle, a corn merchant, died 1850, and his wife Elizabeth Archibald, died 1858, died in New York in 1876. [Kelso gravestone, Roxburghshire]

RAE, JAMES, of Halterburnhead, Yetholm, Roxburghshire, son and heir to James Rae of Halterburnhead who died 20 November 1828. [NRS.S/H]

RAE, JOHN, a skipper in Dunbar, East Lothian, testament, 1824, Comm. Edinburgh. [NRS]

RALSTON, GEORGE, in Philadelphia, Pennsylvania, nephew and heir of John Ralston, the minister in Duns, Berwickshire, 1839. [NRS.S/H]

RAMAGE, ROBERT, a papermaker in Springfield Mill, Mid Lothian, versus Janet Watson, daughter of Thomas Watson a labourer in Bonnyrigg, Mid Lothian, a Process of Divorce in 1808. [NRS.CC8.6.1309]

RAMSAY, ALEXANDER, a butcher in Duns, Berwickshire, married Frances Spears from Berwick-on-Tweed, Northumberland, in Haddington, East Lothian, on 23 November 1795. [NRS.CH12.2.18]

RAMSAY, ALEXANDER, a Lieutenant of the Royal Artillery, third son of Captain Ramsay of the Royal Navy, died in New Orleans, Louisiana, on 1 January 1815. [Inveresk gravestone, Mid Lothian]

RAMSAY, JAMES, a nurseryman in Linlithgow, West Lothian, in 1828. [NRS.CS271.220]

RAMSAY, PETER, son of William Ramsay of Barnton, Mid Lothian, died in Lisbon, Portugal, in 1798. [SM.60.292]

RANKIN, WILLIAM, from Berwick-on-Tweed, Northumberland, emigrated via Greenock aboard the Portaferry to Quebec in May 1832. [QM.13.6.1832]

RATE, GEORGE, of St Mungo's Wells, East Lothian, father of John E. Rate, born 1864, died in Portland, Oregon, on 26 May 1885. [S.13081]

REED, GEORGE, youngest son of George Reed of Hallcross House, Fisher Row, Musselburgh, Mid Lothian, died in St Kitts on 2 September 1860. [S.1663]

REID, CHRISTIAN, a silversmith in Newcastle, Northumberland, eldest son of Andrew Reid a brewer in Canongait, Edinburgh, heir to his cousin

Robert Kerr of Hoselaw, Roxburghshire, son of Robert Kerr of Hoselaw, 7 October 1793; also, heir to his granduncle Andrew Kerr or Reid of Hoselaw, in the barony of Linton, 26 April 1794. [NRS.S/H]

RENNIE, GEORGE, born 1763 in Bo'ness, West Lothian, died on 1 July 1810. [Old Scots gravestone, Charleston, South Carolina]

RENNIE, GEORGE, born 1798, with sister Elizabeth born 1805, and Elizabeth their mother, from Roxburghshire, emigrated on the Brilliant to East Cape Colony, South Africa, in 1820, settled on the Baviaans River. [Scot.Gen.3.1.32]

RENNIE, GEORGE, and his wife Jane, from Haddington, East Lothian, parents of Anna Maria Honora Rennie, born in Rome on 25 July 1826, died there on 5 March 1827. [Protestant Cemetery, Rome]

RENNIE, JOHN, born 1799, from Roxburghshire, emigrated on the Brilliant to East Cape Colony, South Africa, in 1820, settled on the Baviaans River. [Scot.Gen.3.1.32]

RENNIE, JOHN, born 1800, from Roxburghshire, emigrated on the Brilliant to East Cape Colony, South Africa, in 1820, settled on the Baviaans River. [Scot.Gen.3.1.32]

RENTON, HENRY, a minister in Kelso, Roxburghshire, later in Jamaica, son and heir of William Renton a merchant in Edinburgh, 1855. [NRS.S/H]

RENWICK, GEORGE, born 1759, a farmer at Mayshiel, died on 20 January 1833, husband of Anna Henderson born 1760, died 14 February 1836. [Garvald gravestone, East Lothian]

RENWICK, THOMAS, in Buffalo, New York, son and heir of Thomas Renwick a tailor in Hawick, Roxburghshire, 1842. [NRS.S/H]

RENWICK, WILLIAM, born in Roxburghshire, married Jane Jeffrey, settled in New York in 1794 as a merchant. [ANY]

REOCH. JAMES, born 1757 in Leith, a Provost of Leith and Master of the Merchant Company there, died in November 1845. [South Leith gravestone]

REYNOLD, JOHN, son of John Reynold a shoemaker in Tranent, East Lothian, was apprenticed to Adam Keir a baker in Edinburgh on 19 August 1793. [ERA]

RICCALTOUN, ADAM ALEXANDER, sixth son of Reverend John Riccaltoun, of Hobkirk, Roxburghshire, died at Florence Hall, Jamaica, on 18 November 1825. [DPCA.1227] [EEC.17845]

RICHARDSON, ANN, daughter of Thomas Richardson in Linton, Roxburghshire, died in Charleston, South Carolina, in 1796. [NRS.CC8.8.143]

RICHARDSON, JOHN, eldest son of Reverend James Richardson in Morebattle, Roxburghshire, died in Charleston, South Carolina, on 16 March 1818, buried in St Michael's cemetery there. [St Michael's gravestone] [S.71.18]

RICHARDSON, JOHN WHARTON, born 1791 in Berwick, a shipper who died in Middletown, New York on 1 May 1853. [ANY]

RICHARDSON, THOMAS, in Upsetlington boathouse, testament, 1795, Comm. Lauder. [NRS]

RIDDELL, JOHN, born 18 February 1836 in Longformacus, Berwickshire, son of Reverend Henry Riddell and his wife Eliza Horne, settled in Geelong, Victoria, Australia. [F.2.11]

RIDDELL, ROBERT, a mason in Richmond, Virginia, son and heir of Thomas Riddell a mason in Selkirk, Selkirkshire, who died 8 July 1853. [NRS.S/H]

RIDDELL, WILLIAM, a tailor in Canada, son and heir of Walter Riddell a tailor in Hawick, Roxburghshire, who died 11 February 1849. [NRS.S/H]

RIDDELL, WILLIAM born 5 August 1838 in Longformacus, Berwickshire, son of Reverend Henry Riddell and his wife Eliza Horne, settled in Tirhoot, India. [F.2.11]

RIDDELL, ROBERT, a mason in Richmond, Virginia, son and heir of Thomas Riddell, a mason in Selkirk, who died on 8 July 1853. [NRS.S/H]

RIDDELL, THOMAS, born 1776, son of Thomas Riddell of Bessborough, Berwickshire, a Captain of the 14th Regiment, died in Trinidad on 16 September 1802. [Greyfriars gravestone]

RIDDELL, THOMAS, born 1815 in Lilliesleaf, Roxburghshire, emigrated to America in 1820, settled in Lawrence, Massachusetts, husband of Sarah S. Henderson, died 27 December 1862. [HAR]

RIDDELL, WILLIAM, a tailor in Canada, son and heir of Walter Riddell, a tailor in Hawick, Roxburghshire, who died on 11 February 1849. [NRS.S/H]

RIDDLE, WILLIAM, a tailor in Canada West, son and heir of Robert Riddle a merchant in Galashiels, Selkirkshire, 1857. [NRS.S/H]

RIDOUT, JOSEPH, 'born in Berwick, Scotland', in 1774, a mariner who died in Savanna, Georgia, in February 1811. [Savanna Death Register]

RIDPATH, GEORGE, born 1780 in Mid Lothian, died in St John, New Brunswick, on 22 October 1817. [New Brunswick Courier, 25 October 1817]

RINTOUL, ELIZABETH, born 1807, died in New York on 26 March 1869, widow of William Stevenson, born 1795, died 13 January 1842, parents of William, Margaret, and Jane. [Kelso gravestone, Roxburghshire]

RITCHIE, GEORGE, a brewer in Edinburgh, son of Thomas Ritchie a skipper in Leith, trustee for the daughters of Lieutenant John Aire of the Royal Navy, 25 September 1854.

RITCHIE, JAMES, born 20 February 1833, son of Reverend William Ritchie and his wife Isabella Brown in Athelstaneford, East Lothian, died in Switzerland. [F.1.355]

RITCHIE, JOHN, an engineer in Montreal, Quebec, heir to his father John Ritchie a farmer in Blackness, West Lothian, who died on 21 July 1858, 14 August 1889. [NRS.S/H]

ROBB, WILLIAM, born 1790, son of George Robb, [1748-1828], a farmer in Quothquan, and his wife Helen Girdwood, [1749-1834], died in Roanoke, North Carolina, on 16 October 1819. [Skirling gravestone, Peebles-shire]

ROBERTSON, ALEXANDER, born 29 April 1786 in Eddleston, Peebles-shire, son of Reverend Patrick Robertson and his wife Marjory Crawford, a merchant in Florence and Genoa, Italy, died on 26 December 1855. [SGS]

ROBERTSON, ALEXANDER HAMILTON, born 1813, son of Reverend J. M. Robertson in Livingstone, West Lothian, died in St David's, Jamaica, on 5 August 1832. [EEC.18858]

ROBERTSON, ALEXANDER KEITH, born 9 February 1825 in Ladykirk, Berwickshire, son of Reverend George Home Robertson and his wife Elizabeth Kennedy, was killed at Harper's Ferry, West Virginia, in 1865. [F.2.55] NB newspapers claim that he died in Kingston, St Vincent, on 24 February 1845. [AJ.5069][EEC.21155][W.547]

ROBERTSON, CHRISTINA, second daughter of William Robertson a merchant in Dalkeith, Midlothian, married Andrew Aitchison of Jackson, Louisiana, in New Orleans, La., on 27 November 1833. [AJ.4493]

ROBERTSON, DUNDAS, late of Jamaica, died in Musselburgh, Mid Lothian, on 20 September 1822. [SM.90.632]

ROBERTSON, FREDERICK WILLIAM, in Waterloo, Iowa, heir to his grand-aunt Elizabeth Archibald in Portobello, Mid Lothian, who died 4 June 1873. [NRS.S/H]

ROBERTSON, JAMES, a skipper in Bo'ness, West Lothian, testament, 1820, Comm. Edinburgh. [NRS]

ROBERTSON, Reverend JAMES MAITLAND, in Livingston, West Lothian, father of James Robertson, born 1803, died in Trinidad de Cuba, Cuba, on 12 July 1827. [BM.22.768]

ROBERTSON, JAMES, born 1800, son of James Robertson the Adjutant of the Berwickshire Yeomanry Cavalry, died in Jamaica on 20 July 1819. [Duns, Berwickshire, gravestone] [EA]

ROBERTSON, JAMES, late in Jamaica, now in Kelso, Roxburghshire, 1821. [NRS.CC18.4.5.82-106]

ROBERTSON, JAMES, a merchant in Eyemouth, Berwickshire, a decreet, 1831. [NRS.GD267.27.260.4208]

ROBERTSON, JAMES, in Gifford, East Lothian, father of William B. Robertson who died in Calleo, Peru, on 2 October 1877. [S.10709]

ROBERTSON, JOHN PARISH, born in Roxburghshire, emigrated to Argentina in 1813, settled in Monte Grande, near Buenos Ayres, in

1825. [SRP.3]; father of a son born in Valparaiso, Chile, on 17 December 1860. [S.1762]

ROBERTSON, JOHN, from Portobello, Mid Lothian, died in Jamaica on 4 September 1833. [NRS.SC70.1.51]

ROBERTSON, ROBERT, born 1795, an assistant surgeon of the 58th Regiment, died in Jamaica on 18 July 1823. [Kelso gravestone, Roxburghshire]

ROBERTSON, ROBERT, tenant famer in Bluelandhill, Kirknewton, from 1838 to 1843, in Bo'ness Mains from 1843 to 1845, and in Blackcraig near Bangour, West Lothian, from 1845, a journal. [NRS.GD1.994.1]

ROBERTSON, ROBERT JAMES, born 1834, a Writer to the Signet, died in Cannes, France, on 1 May 1867. [Eddleston gravestone, Peebles-shire]

ROBERTSON, THOMAS FAIR, in Hermitage, Kelso, Roxburghshire, and Margaret Lockhart Robertson, there, heirs of their sister Davida Robertson there, 1843. [NRS.S/H]

ROBERTSON, WILLIAM FINDLAY, born in Dalmeny, West Lothian, on 31 December 1786, son of Reverend Thomas Robertson and his wife Jane Jackson, a Lieutenant in the Service of the Honourable East India Company. [F.I.202]

ROBERTSON, WILLIAM, in Coldstream, Berwickshire, a Lieutenant Commander of the Royal Navy, testament, 1813, Comm. Lauder. [NRS]

ROBERTSON, Reverend WILLIAM, born 1798, from Haddington, East Lothian, a missionary of the Secession Church of Scotland, died in Canada on 22 September 1832. [FH.560]

ROBERTSON, WILLIAM, born 2 September 1792 in Eddleston, Peebles-shire, son of Reverend Patrick Robertson and his wife Margaret Crawford, a merchant in Leghorn alias Livorno, Italy, died on 11 July 1861. [SGS]

ROBINSON, DOUGLAS, youngest son of William Ross Robinson in Clermiston, married Fanny Monroe, eldest daughter of James Monroe in Fanwood, New York, there on 14 November 1850. [W.XL.1174]

ROBINSON, JOHN HEY, in Elleslie, Baltimore, Maryland, heir to his grand-aunt Janet Duncan in Newbigging, Musselburgh, Mid Lothian, who died on 10 June 1865. [NRS.S/H]

ROBSON, ALEXANDER, son of James Robson in Chatto, was apprenticed to Bell, Wardrop, and Russell, surgeons in Edinburgh, for five years, on 29 November 1799. [ERA]

ROBSON, Reverend JAMES, born 1775 in Kelso, Roxburghshire, a minister in Lochwinnoch, Renfrewshire, emigrated to Nova Scotia in 1811, a minister in Halifax, N.S., from 1812 to 1817, Clerk of the Synod of Nova Scotia from 1817 until his death on 8 December 1838. [HPC]

ROGERS, JAMES, probably from Roxburghshire, a shopkeeper in Charleston, South Carolina, probate on 1 August 1794, S.C.

RODGER, JAMES, in Cincinnatti, Ohio, grandson and heir to James Rodger a tailor in Tranent, East Lothian, who died 6 January 1845. [NRS.S/H]

RODGER, JOHN, son of John Rodger a gardener at Cramond, West Lothian, was apprenticed to John Morrison a barber in Edinburgh on 5 October1797. [ERA]

ROMANES, JAMES, son of John Romanes a burgess of Lauder, was apprenticed to Forrester and Company, merchants in Edinburgh, for five years, on 29 November 1799. [ERA]

ROSS, or DEWAR, FANNY, in Oshawa, Canada, daughter and heir of James Ross in Blainlie, Roxburghshire, who died on 25 February 1832. [NRS.S/H]

ROSS, D.M., in Poltonbank, Lasswade, Mid Lothian, formerly a Captain of the 34th Regiment of Foot, applied to settle in Canada on 26 May 1819. [TNA.CO.384]

ROSS, G. C., second son of Alexander Ross in Morham, Haddington, East Lothian, died at Aux Cayes, Haiti, on 24 November 1866. [S.7308]

ROSS, JAMES ROBERTSON, in Oshawa, Canada, grandson and heir of James Ross in Blainslie, Roxburghshire, who died on 25 February 1832. [NRS.S/H]

ROSS, ROBERT, born 1775, son of Robert Ross, [1720-1810]. A farmer in Greatlaws, and his wife Helen Henderson, [1746-1818], died in Jamaica in 1813. [Skirling gravestone, Peebles-shire]

ROUGHEAD, WILLIAM, a merchant in Haddington, East Lothian, records, 1800-1815. [NRS.CS96.823]

ROWE, RALPH, born 1847, third son of William Hutton Rowe a surgeon in Coldstream, Berwickshire, died in Chillan, Chile, on 5 February 1869. [S.8009]

ROY, JAMES, of Nenthorn, Berwickshire, died in Philadelphia, Pennsylvania, on 1 July 1836. [AJ.4622]

RULE, JOHN, born in Kelso, Roxburghshire, the Shipping Officer of Halifax, Nova Scotia, died on 29 May 1827. [BM.22.528]

RUSSELL, JOSEPH, born 1828, died in Castlemaine, Australia, on 21 February 1865. [Merton gravestone, Berwickshire]

RUTHERFORD, GEORGE, born 1816, son of Thomas Rutherford, [1773-1835], and his wife Margaret Hay, [1776-1837], died in New York on 13 July 1835. [Westruther gravestone, Berwickshire]

RUTHERFORD, JAMES, a former tenant in Longnewton, Roxburghshire, died on St Kitts on 28 November 1818. [EA.5748.71]

RUTHERFORD, JAMES, born 1819, a coachman, died in Kelso on 13 November 1863, husband of Elizabeth Rae, born 1825, died on 1 July 1893. [Kelso, Roxburghshire, gravestone]

RUTHERFORD, JOHN CHATTO, youngest son of William Oliver Rutherford of Edgerton, Roxburghshire, died in Crewzuach, Rhenish Prussia, Germany, on 4 July 1857. [W.XVIII.1889

RUTHERFORD, THOMAS, jr., a merchant in Sheffield, Yorkshire, England, eldest son of Andrew Rutherford a merchant in Jedburgh, Roxburghshire, died in Christianstad, St Croix, Danish West Indies, on 22 November 1808. [SM.71.398] [EA.4750]

RUTHERFORD, THOMAS, of Fairnington, Roxburghshire, brother and heir of Charles Rutherford who died 11 July 1846, 1846. [NRS.S/H]

RUTHERFORD, WALTER, from New Edgarston, Roxburghshire, died in New York on 9 January 1804. [DPCA.86]

RUTHERFORD, WALTER B., born in Jedburgh, Roxburghshire, emigrated to America in 1815, was naturalised in South Carolina on 16 April 1819. [S.C. Citizenship Book.82]

RUTHERFORD, WILLIAM, a shoemaker in Kelso, Roxburghshire, heir to his father George Rutherford in Kelso, 20 March 1790. [NRS.S/H]

RUTHERFORD, WILLIAM ELDER, in Newton near Melrose, Roxburghshire, son and heir of Reverend William Rutherford, 1846. [NRS.S/H]

SADDLER, JOHN, a carpenter in Dunbar, East Lothian, was accused of rioting in Dunbar in 1816. [NRS.SC40.54.1.32]

SAMSON, JOHN, a shipmaster in Queensferry, West Lothian, testament, 1814, Comm. Edinburgh. [NRS]

SANDERSON, ALEXANDER, a builder in Dalkeith, Mid Lothian, a bond in 1822. [NRS.GD81.313]

SANDERSON, JOHN, a manufacturer in Canada West, nephew and heir of John Sanderson, a shoemaker in Galashiels, Selkirkshire, who died on 30 April 1847. [NRS.S/H]

SANGSTER, Reverend JOHN, born in the Manse of Humbie on 11 January 1768, ordained at Garvald on 2 April 1800, died in Haddington, East Lothian, on 10 October 1855, husband of Margaret Hay, who died on 23 January 1833. [Garvald gravestone, East Lothian]

SCHOOLER, JAMES, born 1823 in Hutton, Berwickshire, son of John Schooler, a feuar in Paxton, Berwickshire, and his wife Isabella Knox, settled in California, died 11 April 1883. [Hutton gravestone]

SCOON, JOHN, born 27 April 1771 in Hawick, Roxburghshire, settled in Geneva, New York, in 1820, husband of Margaret Renwick, died 26 January 1861. [BAF]

SCOTLAND, R. B., died in Yokahama, Japan, on 22 January 1869. [Kailzie gravestone, Peebles-shire]

SCOTLAND, THOMAS, born 1823, died in Macao, China, on 10 July 1844. [Kailzie gravestone, Peebles-shire]

SCOTT, AGNES, spouse of William Johnston a candlemaker in Musselburgh, Mid Lothian, versus Alexander Harper a shoemaker in Tranent, East Lothian, a Process of Scandal, 1823. [NRS.CC8.6.205]

SCOTT, ALISON ERSKINE, youngest daughter of Ebenezer Scott a surgeon in Dalkeith, Midlothian, married W. G. Adams a merchant in Memphis, Tennessee, there on 18 January 1839. [EEC.19874]

SCOTT, ANDREW, born 25 March 1804 in Penicuik, Mid Lothian, a merchant in Kingston, Jamaica, for 37 years, died in London on 10 May 1857, buried in Glasgow Necropolis. [St Andrew's Presbyterian Church, Jamaica, plaque]

SCOTT, ANNE, wife of Charles Baillie of Jerviswood, Roxburghshire, letters, 1822-1838. [NRS.GD157.244]

SCOTT, ARCHIBALD, from the Scottish Borders, settled in Canada, a letter to his cousin in Scotland dated about 1845. [NRS.GD1.813.17]

SCOTT, CHARLES, third son of Francis Scott of Harden, died in Jamaica in 1805. [AJ.3029]

SCOTT, CHARLES ANDREW, of Bridgeheugh, born 1817, eldest son of William and Alice Scott of Woll, Roxburghshire, died in Rome on 7 April 1838. [Protestant Cemetery, Rome]; inventory, 1839. [NRS]

SCOTT, DAVID, born 23 December 1779 in Haddington, East Lothian, son of Reverend Robert Scott and his wife Margaret Sheriff, a surgeon in the East India Service, died 4 June 1816 in India. [F.I.373]

SCOTT, DAVID, born 1854, son of Jacob Scott and his wife Isabella Hogg, died in Dunedin, Otago, New Zealand, on 7 June 1879. [Coldstream gravestone, Berwickshire]

SCOTT, Major FRANCIS, second son of John Scott of Whitehaugh, Roxburghshire, died at San Sebastian, Spain, in 1813. [SM.75.799]

SCOTT, HARRIET, of Harden, Berwickshire, a letter from Prince Adam Czaroryski, in 1833. [NRS.GD157.2455]

SCOTT, JAMES HARPER, born 1857, died in Origaba, Mexico, on 20 March 1888. [Greenlaw gravestone, Berwickshire]

SCOTT, JEAN, born 1801 in Lauder, Berwickshire, wife of Joseph Hardie, died in Turra Vale, Melbourne, Australia, on 4 August 1859. [Lauder gravestone]

SCOTT, JOHN, son of Alexander Scott a skinner in Dalkeith, Mid Lothian, was apprenticed to David Gray a skinner in Edinburgh on 7 August 1794. [ERA]

SCOTT, JOHN, was found guilty in Jedburgh, Roxburghshire, of stealing sheep, and was sentenced to transportation to the colonies for fourteen years, on 10 April 1826. [SM.86.638]

SCOTT, Dr JOHN, from the Scottish Borders, a physician in Ontario, a letter to his cousin Andrew Redford in Hermiston, Mid Lothian, dated 1840. [NRS.GD1.813.4]

SCOTT, Reverend JOHN, was ordained in Jedburgh, Roxburghshire, emigrated to Nova Scotia in 1826, minister of St Matthew's in Halifax, N.S., from 1827 until 1863, died in February 1864. [HPC]

SCOTT, JOHN, born 1826, died in St Louis, Missouri, on 3 January 1873. [Kelso gravestone, Roxburghshire]

SCOTT, ROBERT, from Hawick, Roxburghshire, a theological student who emigrated to Canada in the 1820s. [UPC]

SCOTT, ROBERT, a cabinetmaker in Boston, Massachusetts, son and heir of William Scott, a slater in Hawick, Roxburghshire, who died on 3 February 1866. [NRS.S/H]

SCOTT, ROBERT, a saddler in Scotland, Oakland, California, brother and heir to Isabella Scott in Jedburgh, Roxburghshire, who died on24 July 1867. [NRS.S/H]

SCOTT, STEPHEN, MD, son of John Scott a farmer in Limpetlaw, Kelso, Roxburghshire, died in Georgetown, Demerara, on 19 March 1872. [S.8961]

SCOTT, THOMAS, "sometime in Van Diemen's land", died in Earlston, Berwickshire, on 3 March 1855. [Earlston gravestone, Berwickshire]

SCOTT, WALTER, born 1817, son of Walter Scott of Wauchope, Roxburghshire, a surgeon in the Service of the East India Company, died in Allahabad, Bengal, India, on 17 August 1844. [Allahabad gravestone]

SCOTT, WILLIAM, son of Dr John Scott of Coats, formerly a merchant in Madeira, died in Loanhead, Mid Lothian, on 23 September 1809. [EA.XCII.4773]

SCOTT, WILLIAM, from Ettrickbank, Selkirk, late in Jamaica, died on 21 April 1820. [S.4.168]

SCOTT, WILLIAM, born 1784, son of William Scott of Wooler, Roxburghshire, died in Quebec on 13 January 1820. [AR.19.2.1820]

SCOTT, WILLIAM, born 8 April 1783 in Haddington, East Lothian, son of Reverend Robert Scott and his wife Margaret Sheriff, a surgeon in Madras, India, died 14 March 1866. [F.1.373]

SCOTT, WILLIAM, born 1813, a missionary in Jamaica, died on 14 August 1841, son of William Scott in Garvald Mains [1785-1869], and his wife Janet Black, [[1780-1864]. [Garvald gravestone, East Lothian]

SCOTT, WILLIAM, in New York, son and heir of Walter Scott, a weaver in Hawick, Roxburghshire, later in Dovemount, in 1845. [NRS.S/H]

SCOUGALL, JAMES, in Sheriffhall, East Lothian, a victim of theft and arson in 1849. [NRS. AD14 49.104]

SCOULAR, DAVID, agent for the Edinburgh and Glasgow Bank in Midcalder, West Lothian, in 1849. [POD]

SCOULER, THOMAS, born 1765 in Haddington, East Lothian, a ships carpenter in Charleston, South Carolina, was naturalised in Charleston on 26 June 1812. [NARA.M1183.1]

SEMPLE, THOMAS, a butcher in Berwick-on-Tweed, Northumberland, married Jane Robertson of the same parish, in Haddington, East Lothian, on 19 January 1792. [NRS.CH12.2.18]

SHAIRP, CHARLES MORDAUNT, born 3 August 1810 in Bathgate, West Lothian, son of William Shairp of Kirkton, a Customs Collector, and his wife Eustatia David, to India in 1829, a Lieutenant of the Bengal Army, died at Etawah on 24 October 1841. [BA.4.57]

SHAIRP, NORMAN, born 20 October 1779, son of Thomas Shairp of Houston, West Lothian, and his wife Mary McLeod, to India in 1800, a

Captain of the 12th Native Infantry of the Bengal Army, died on 7 April 1864. [BA.4.58]

SHAIRP, NORMAN, jr., was appointed Deputy Lieutenant of West Lothian in 1825. [NRS.GD30.905]

SHAIRP, THOMAS, of Houstoun, granted a tack [lease] to James Cunningham a farmer in Houston, Uphall, West Lothian, for 99 years, in 1826. [NRS.GD30.708]

SHAIRP, WILLIAM, son of Major Shairp in Bo'ness, West Lothian, settled in New South Wales, Australia, in 1825, a letter dated 1845. [NRS.GD314.110]

SHAND, WILLIAM, in Jefferson County, Ohio, son and heir of John Shand, a tenant farmer in Wolfstar, East Lothian, who died on 14 November 1859. [NRS.S/H]

SHARP, LAURENCE, a shipmaster in Dunbar, East Lothian, testament, 1822, Comm. Edinburgh. [NRS]

SHARP, WILLIAM, in the west end of Queensferry, West Lothian, to appear before the Sheriff of Linlithgow on 15 February 1800. [NRS.GD75.64]

SHAW, WILLIAM, born 1848 in Bo'ness, West Lothian, died in Port Elizabeth, South Africa, on 20 September 1922. [St George gravestone, Port Elizabeth, Cape of Good Hope]

SHERIFF, JANE CHRISTIE, born 29 December 1831 in Fala, Mid Lothian, son of Reverend Thomas Sheriff and his wife Janet McEwan, died in Australia in October 1880. [F.I.319]

SHERIFF, JOHN LIDDLE, born 19 November 1829 in Fala, Mid Lothian, son of Reverend Thomas Sheriff and his wife Janet McEwan, a bookseller, died in Sydney, New South Wales, Australia, in May 1882. [F.I.319]

SHIELS, ALEXANDER, a farmer in Kedzlie, [1818-1868], and his wife Sybella Smith, [1830-1851], parents of James Shiels who settled in Texas. [Earlston gravestone, Berwickshire]

SHIELLS, MAY or MARION, in Whittleknow near Spotswood, Westruther, Berwickshire, versus her husband James Somerville, a planter on Forrest Estate, Westmoreland, Cornwall County, Jamaica, eldest son of John Somerville of Jenlaw, a Process of Divorce in 1794. Comm. Edinburgh. [NRS]

SHIELLS, WILLIAM, a nurseryman in Dalkeith, Mid Lothian, papers, 1804-1835. [NRS.GD224.482.1]

SIBBALD, JOHN, a joiner in Crosslee, Roxburghshire, son and heir of Andrew Sibbald, son of John Sibbald portioner of Eildon, 1847. [NRS.S/H]

SIM, JOHN, of Cartmore, was admitted as a burgess of Queensferry, West Lothian, on 2 July 1802. [NRS.GD172.404]

SIMPSON, JOHN, a sailor in Grangepans, West Lothian, was accused of poaching in 1825. [NRS.B48.16.6.6]

SIMPSON, ROBERT, born 1817, son of James Simpson, [1785-1856], and his wife Helen Williamson, [1780-1869], died in Boston on 10 June 1841. [Cramond gravestone, West Lothian]

SIMPSON, THOMAS B., in Lauder, Peebles-shire, a Captain in the Royal Navy, inventory, 1822, Comm. Lauder. [NRS]

SINCLAIR, JAMES, born 11 July 1827, son of Thomas Sinclair and his wife Margaret Robertson in Penicuik, Mid Lothian, settled in Newhaven, Connecticut in 1855. [SI.409]

SINCLAIR, THOMAS B., from Lauder, Peebles-shire, a Captain of the Royal Navy, inventory, 1822, Comm. Lauder. [NRS]

SKED, JOHN, born 24 March 1755, a baker, died on 18 March 1825, husband of Euphemia White, born 1756, died 18 October 1837. [Innerwick gravestone, East Lothian]

SKEILL, DAVID, ELEANOR, and MARY, children of James Skeill a farmer and feuar in Musselburgh, Mid Lothian, 3 August 1795. [NRS.CS97.111.150]

SKELDON, GEORGE, born 1776, died 2 August 1853, husband of Mary Nelson, born 1790, died 2 August 1884. [Oldhamstocks gravestone, East Lothian]

SKIERLAW, DAVID, a cooper in Eyemouth, Berwickshire, testament, 1792, Comm. Lauder. [NRS]

SMART, WILLIAM, born 1788 in Haddington, East Lothian, son of Alexander Smart, emigrated to Canada in 1811, a minister in Upper Canada, died in Ganenoque on 9 September 1876. [F.]

SMEATON, ELIZABETH, born 1809, from the Grange, Morebattle, Roxburghshire, relict of George Clark in Rostrevor, County Down, Ireland, died at Beach Road, the Thames, Auckland, New Zealand, on 3 June 1884. [S.12812]

SMITH, ELIZABETH ROWAND, daughter of Reverend William Smith in Musselburgh, married the Reverend Thomas Langhorn, in Musselburgh, Midlothian, on 23 September 1822. [SM.90.520]

SMITH, JAMES, born 1836, son Reverend James Smith and his wife Agnes Fyfe, died in Aleppo, Syria, on 17 November 1857. [Kelso gravestone, Roxburghshire]

SMITH, JANET, relict of Robert Wright a baker in Haddington, East Lothian, versus her spouse Thomas Lithgow, formerly the Quartermaster of the Windsor Foresters Regiment, a Process of Separation and Aliment in 1803. [NRS.CC8.6.1178]

SMITH, JOHN, a wright and portioner in Darnick, Roxburghshire, heir to his father Andrew Smith a portioner there, 8 April 1790. [NRS.S/H]

SMITH, JOHN, born 1786 in Ancrum, Roxburghshire, was accused of jail-breaking in 1816. [NRS.AD14.16.16]

SMITH, JOHN, in Berbice, appointed his parents Thomas Smith and his wife Janet Frew in Bathgate, West Lothian, as his attornies, subscribed in New Amsterdam, Berbice, a deed dated 31 May 1815. [NRS.RD5.160.367]

SMITH, JOHN, born 1807, died in Tarbolton, Ontario, on 24 November 1879. [Duns gravestone, Berwickshire]

SMITH, JOHN FYFFE, born 26 February 1838 in Kelso, Roxburghshire, son of Reverend James Smith and his wife Agnes Fyffe, died in Tangiers, Morocco, on 8 July 1858. [F.2.73] [Kelso gravestone]

SMITH, MARGARET, fourth daughter of Alexander Smith in Dunbar, East Lothian, married Walter Denholm, on the Estancia San Juan Paysandu in Monte Video, Uruguay, on 5 October 1868. [S.7910]

SMITH, THOMAS, a tailor in Bo'ness, West Lothian, versus John Cameron in Edinburgh, a decreet, 1830. [NRS.CS46.1830.2.3]

SMITH, WILLIAM, with two nephews, from Haddington, East Lothian, emigrated via Greenock aboard the Portaferry bound for Quebec in May 1832. [QM.13.6.1832] [GWS]

SNADDON, JOHN, in Newton of Bo'ness, West Lothian, was accused of non-payment of revenue in 1825. [NRS.B48.16.6.6]

SNEDDAN, JAMES, a sailor in Bo'ness, West Lothian, in 1793. [NRS.S/H]

SOMERVILLE, ALEXANDER, born 1772 in Roxburghshire, son of Dr Archibald Somerville, a bookseller in New York by 1798, died in New Orleans, Louisiana, on 4 September 1804. [ANY]

SOMERVILLE, DAVID, born in April 1742 in Currie, Mid Lothian, son of John Somerville and his wife Margaret Cunningham, emigrated to South Carolina in1790, a minister in Charleston, died there in 1792. [NRS.CC8.8.131] [Colonial Families.3.534]

SOMERVILLE, WILLIAM, son of John Somerville, [1754-1811], a farmer in Bonnington, and his wife Janet, [1753-1808], died in Clear Creeks County, Indiana, on 7 September 1821. [Peebles gravestone]

SOMMERVILLE, WILLIAM, was accused of culpable and furious driving a cart in Currie, Mid Lothian, in 1825. [NRS.AD14.25.36]

SOMERVILLE, WILLIAM, born 22 April 1771 in Minto, Roxburghshire, died in Florence, Italy, on 25 June 1860. [Florence gravestone]

SOUNESS, JAMES, born 1801, from Roxburghshire, emigrated on the Brilliant to East Cape Colony, South Africa, in 1820, settled on the Baviaans River. [Scot.Gen.3.1.32]

SPARK, MARY HYMES, born 1822, daughter of John Spark and his wife Mary Hymes, died in Melbourne, Australia, on 26 November 1890. [Westruther gravestone, Berwickshire]

SPEEDIN, THOMAS, in Bowden, Roxburghshire, son and heir of William Speedin, a portioner born 1820, 24 January 1793. [NRS.S/H]

STEIN, ANDREW, and Company, distillers in Kirkliston, West Lothian, sederunt books, 1831-1835. [NRS.CS96185.1/2]

SPENCE, ALEXANDER, a merchant in Duns, Berwickshire, a bankrupt who absconded to America around 1796. [NRS.CS23.Seqn.2/3]

SPENCE, GEORGE, son of William Spence a farmer at Musselburgh, Mid Lothian, was apprenticed to Archibald Anderson a merchant in Edinburgh on 12 October 1795. [ERA]

SPENCE, WILLIAM, son of William Spence a farmer at Musselburgh, Mid Lothian, was apprenticed to Alexander Cunningham a baker in Edinburgh on 12 October 1795. [ERA]

SPOUSE, WILLIAM, a baker in Coldingham, Berwickshire, testament, 1791, Comm. Lauder. [NRS]

SPROT, JAMES, of Sprot, born 14 January 1804, Deputy Lieutenant of the County of Haddington, died on 5 July 1882, husband of Mary Watt born 16 February 1817, died on 17 January 1881. [Spott gravestone]

STALKER, DONALD, in America, son and heir of Marion Davidson or Stalker in Peebles, Peebles-shire, 1844. [NRS.S/H]

STEEDMAN, THOMAS, from Penicuik, Mid Lothian, a soldier of the Caithness Highland Regiment, versus his wife Isobel Brown, daughter of George Brown formerly a soldier in the Elgin Fencibles, residing at the foot of Leith Wynd, Edinburgh, in 1804. [NRS.CC8.6.1188]

STEEL, JAMES, born 1742, was ordained in Cockpen, Midlothian, in 1768, emigrated to Jamaica in 1787, died on 17 February 1790. [BHF]

STEEL, JAMES, born 1793, a prisoner in Jedburgh Tollbooth, Roxburghshire, was accused of jailbreaking in 1816. [NRS.AD14.16.16]

STEEL, WALTER, born 1799, from Peebles, died in Madeira on 21 November 1831. [ARM]

STENHOUSE, JOHN, born 1799, died 12 March 1851, husband of Jessie Stevenson, born 1800, died 20 February 1877. [Eccles gravestone, Berwickshire]

105

STEUART, PETER, born 1773, son of Robert Steuart and his wife Janet Robertson, died in Jamaica in 1815. [Eccles gravestone, Berwickshire]

STEVEN, WILLIAM, messenger at arms, Bathgate, West Lothian, 1849. [POD]

STEVENSON, ALEXANDER, son of Reverend David Stevenson in Wilton, Roxburghshire, an assistant colonial surgeon, died in Sierra Leone on 18 April 1841. [AJ.4865]

STEVENSON, HAY, born in the Borders, a merchant in New York from 1783, married Jessie Graham on 29 July 1790, parents of John Graham Stevenson, died on 24 September 1799. [ANY]

STEVENSON, JANE, eldest daughter of Reverend David Stevenson in Wilton, Roxburghshire, married James Favish a merchant in Montreal, Quebec, at Wilton Manse on 31 August 1840. [EEC.20098]

STEVENSON, JOHN, master of the sloop Otter of London, married Heen Booth from Peterhead, Aberdeenshire, in Haddington, East Lothian, on 9 October 1791. [NRS.CH12.2.2.18]

STEVENSON, JOHN, born in Melrose, Roxburghshire, proprietor of the 'Guiana Chronicle', in Georgetown, Demerara, was drowned in the Orinocco River on 25 August 1823. [BM.15.492]

STEVENSON, THOMAS, born 4 September 1854 in Melrose, Roxburghshire, died in South Africa on 28 March 1922. [St George gravestone, Port Elizabeth, Cape of Good Hope]

STEWART, ANDREW, son of John Stewart at Dalhousie, Mid Lothian, was apprenticed to Mark Kerr a printer in Edinburgh on 1 July 1790. [ERA]

STEWART, ARCHIBALD, born 1769, possibly from Queensferry, West Lothian, a merchant in Halifax, Nova Scotia, died 12 January 1835, probate 19 December 1835, Halifax, N.S.

STEWART, CHARLES, son of James Stewart in Haddington, East Lothian, was apprenticed for six years to Edward Simpson a barber in Edinburgh on 21 June 1792. [ERA]

STEWART, DUNCAN, a surgeon in Bo'ness, West Lothian, a decreet in 1830. [NRS.CS46.1830.2.20]

STEWART, KATHERINE, spouse of George Bayne, a mason formerly in Dunbar, East Lothian, later a potter at Leith Gas Works, versus the said George Bayne, a divorce, 1803. [NRS.CC8.6,1239]

STRATTON, JOHN, in Cambridge, New York, son and heir of Peter Stratton a carrier in Lilliesleaf, Roxburghshire, 1820. [NRS.SH]

STRAUCHAN, JOHN, born 1761, parochial schoolmaster of Swinton, Berwickshire, died on 16 March 1840, his relict Cecilia Rae, died in Sydenham, Owen Sound, Canada West, on 1 June 185-. [Swinton gravestone]

STUART, W., agent of the British Linen Company in Peebles in 1849. [POD]

SUTTIE, Sir GEORGE GRANT, in Sheriffhall, East Lothian, a victim of theft and arson in 1849. [NRS. AD14 49.104]

SWAN, HENRY, a writer in Kelso, Roxburghshire, in 1816. [NRS.AD30.9]

SWAN, JOHN, from Jedburgh, Roxburghshire, studied theology and medicine around 1806, settled in America as a surgeon. [UPC] in Huntsvill, USA, on 4 April 1877. [Ednam gravestone, Roxburghshire]

SWANSON, JOHN GOODFELLOW, a rigger in San Francisco, California, son and heir of Janet Goodfellow, wife of Donald Swanson in Langside, Peebles, 1867. [NRS.S/H]

SWANSTON, or OVENS, AGNES, in Montreal, Quebec, daughter and heir of John Swanston, a mason in Newton, St Boswells, Roxburghshire, in 1843. [NRS.S/H]

SWANSTON, ANDREW, born 1830, son of Robert Swanston, died in Barbados on 16 June 1836. [Greenlaw gravestone, Berwickshire]

SWANSTON, JAMES, in Marshall Meadows, Berwickshire, father of Helen Swanston who died in St Kitts on 16 February 1869. [S.7999]

SWANSTON, or BAIN, MARGARET, in Montreal, Quebec, daughter and heir of John Swanston, a mason in Newton, St Boswells, Roxburghshire, in 1843. [NRS.S/H]

SWANSTON, WILLIAM, son of John Swanston in Haddington, East Lothian, a surgeon in St Kitts, appointed John Swanston in Haddington as his attorney on 23 April 1796, [NRS.RD3.276/293]; a sasine in 1802. [NRS.RS.Shetland .452]

SWINTON, H., a merchant in Grangemouth, West Lothian, and his wife Jean Steel, parents of George Steel Swinton who settled in the Sandwich Islands [Hawaii], before 1847. [NRS.S/H]

SWINTON, JESSIE, relict of Peter Logan a farmer at Duncanlaw, died at Niagara, Canada West, on 29 November 1858. [W.XIX.2044]

SYDSERF, CHARLES, born 1798, from Roxburghshire, emigrated on the Brilliant to East Cape Colony, South Africa, in 1820, settled on the Baviaans River. [Scot.Gen.3.1.32]

SYMINGTON, HENRY, a merchant in Penicuik, Mid Lothian, father of John Symington, born 1852, died in Wellington, New Zealand, in June 1884. [S.12843]

TAIT, DAVID, in Quebec, brother and heir of James Tait in Lauder, Berwickshire, who died on 24 January 1867. [NRS.S/H]

TAIT, DAVID, eldest son of John Tait an innkeeper in Aberlady, East Lothian, of the Law Stamp Office, died in Montreal on 25 March 1877. [EC.28880]

TAIT, ELIZABETH, wife of Charles Douglas in Jedburgh, Roxburghshire, was accused of rioting and assault at Jedburgh Tollhouse in 1829. [NRS.AD14.29.210]

TAIT, JACOB, a mug selling tinker in Kirk Yetholm, Dumfries-shire, was accused of rioting and assault at Jedburgh Tollhouse, Roxburghshire, in 1829. [NRS.AD14.29.210]

TAIT, DAVID, in Quebec, brother and heir of James Tait in Lauder, Berwickshire, who died on 24 January 1867. [NRS.S/H]

TAIT, EUPHEMIA, from Cramond, Mid Lothian, wife of John Pryde, a collier at Edgehead Mill, was accused of murder in 1838. [NRS.AD14.38.513]

TAIT, JAMES HILL, born 31 August 1835, son of Reverend Adam Duncan Tait in Kirkliston, West Lothian, was educated at Edinburgh University, ordained in Linlithgow, West Lothian, in 1861, an Anglican chaplain in France and Italy, died in Rome on 18 April 1900. [F.1.353]
108

TAIT, JAMES, agent in Kelso, Roxburghshire, for the National Bank of Scotland in 1849. [POD]

TAIT, PETER, born 1781, a tenant farmer in Horndean, husband of Agnes Hogarth, [1779-1817], died in Chicago, Illinois, on 18 May 1836. [Whitsome gravestone, Berwickshire]

TAIT, ROBERT, from Haddington, settled in Elisabethtown, North Carolina, married Miss E. B. Vert, also from Haddington, East Lothian, in New York on 17 February 1855. [EEC.22710]

TAYLOR, ALEXANDER, son of George Taylor a brewer in Linlithgow, West Lothian, was apprenticed to William Murray a baker in Edinburgh on 29 November 1800. [ERA]

TAYLOR, COLIN FALCONER, eldest son of the Rector of Musselburgh Grammar School, Mid Lothian, died in Hamilton, Bermuda, on 3 September 1818. [BM.4.381][S.2.97]

TAYLOR, EDWARD WILGRESS, born 26 January 1843, son of Reverend John Taylor and his wife Eleanor Kay Hick, was drowned of the Cape of Good Hope, South Africa, on 13 March 1859. [Drumelzier gravestone, Peebles-shire] [F.1.270]

TAYLOR, JOHN, from Kelso, Roxburghshire, a tailor in Troy, New York, son and heir of William Taylor, a tailor in Kelso, 1832. [NRS.S/H]

TAYLOR, PETER, a quarryman in Swineburn, Kirkliston, West Lothian, was accused of night poaching with an offensive weapon there, in 1830. [NRS.AD14.30.260]

TAYLOR, WILLIAM, First Lieutenant of the Royal Linlithgow Volunteers, was admitted as a burgess and guilds-brother of Dunfermline, Fife, on 15 August 1804. [DM]

TELFER, JANE and ELIZA, in Kelso, Roxburghshire, heirs to their father Andrew Telfer a bookseller in Kelso, 1845. [NRS.S/H]

TELFER, WILLIAM, from Hawick, Roxburghshire, a wright in Canada, son and heir of Isabel Nichol or Telfer, in 1844. [NRS.S/H]

TELFORD, MARGARET, daughter of Robert Telford a weaver in Kelso, Roxburghshire, now in Dalkeith, Mid Lothian, a Process of Divorce versus Henry McMillan, Adjutant of the Royal Scots Greys in 1804. [NRS.CC8.6.1186]

TELLFORD, ROBERT, born 1773, a lapidary in Leitholm, died 8 December 1846, husband of Agnes Glasgow, born 1789, died 25 May 1867. [Eccles gravestone, Berwickshire]

TEMPLETON, HELEN, born 1820, a servant from Roxburghshire, emigrated on the White Star bound for Hobart, Tasmania, Australia, in 1855. [SRA.TD292]

TENANT, MARY, spouse to Andrew Fyvie a vintner in Musselburgh, versus Thomas Legat a tanner in Musselburgh, Mid Lothian, a Process of Scandal, 1798. [NRS.CC8.6.1038]

TELFER, WILLIAM, from Hawick, Roxburghshire, a wright in Canada, son and heir of Isabel Nichol or Telfer, 1844. [NRS.S/H]

THOMSON, AGNES, daughter of George Thomson in America, wife of William Alexander in Cockenzie, East Lothian, died in Tranent, East Lothian, on 26 January 1848. [SG.1686]

THOMSON, ALEXANDER, son of James Thomson a miller at Stockbridge, was apprenticed to James Spence, a barber in Edinburgh, for six and a half years, on 17 June 1790. [ERA]

THOMSON, ALEXANDER, eldest son of James Thomson in Oatridge, Linlithgow, West Lothian, died in Jamaica in December 1819. [BM.6.727]

THOMSON, ANDREW, son of Thomas Thomson a clerk in the Cess Office, was apprenticed to Thomas Stuart, a white iron smith in Edinburgh, for six years on 23 June 1791. [ERA]

THOMSON, EDWARD, born 19 April 1821 in Duddingston, Mid Lothian, son of Reverend John Thomson and his wife Frances Ingram Spence, emigrated to Australia. [F.1.20]

THOMSON, GEORGE, in St Louis, North America, brother and heir of Jane Thomson in High Buckholmside, Galashiels, Selkirkshire, who died on 19 April 1863. [NRS.S/H]

THOMSON, HENRY FRANCIS, born 3 August 1819 in Duddingston, Mid Lothian, son of Reverend John Thomson and his wife Frances Ingram Spence, a coffee planter in Ceylon, died there. [F.1.20]

THOMSON, HENRY JAMES, of Allerly, in Jedburgh, Roxburghshire, son and heir of Alexander Thomson formerly a stationer in Jedburgh, Roxburghshire,1847. [NRS.S/H]

THOMSON, JAMES, a fisherman in Newhaven, Midlothian, in 1799. [NRS.S/H]

THOMSON, JAMES, born 1760, a shepherd at Castle Moffat, died on 22 April 1844, husband of Martha Messer, born 1764, died 3 September 1850. [Garvald gravestone, East Lothian]

THOMSON, JAMES, son of James Thomson a labourer in Common Close, Dalkeith, Midlothian, was accused of prison breaking in 1821. [NRS.AD14.21.220]

THOMSON, JAMES, a slater in Dalkeith, Mid Lothian, a thief imprisoned in Haddington Tolbooth, trial papers, 1822. [NRS.SC40.54.2.7]

THOMSON, JAMES, a wright in Jedburgh, Roxburghshire, son and heir of John Thomson a farmer at Crichton Dean, 1840. [NRS.S/H]

THOMSON, JANET, youngest daughter of James Thomson of Earnshaw, married Dr C. Wightman, late physician in Alnwick, Northumberland, at Bogend, Duns, Berwickshire, on 22 October 1822. [SM.90.631]

THOMSON, or INGLIS, MARGARET, in Linton, Roxburghshire, sister and heir of James Thomson in Jamaica, in 1833. [NRS.S/H]

THOMSON, ROBERT, second son of Thomas Thomson the town-clerk of Musselburgh, Mid Lothian, a surgeon who died in Demerara on 6 February 1821. [BM.9.245][EA]

THOMPSON, ROBERT, born 1826, son of John Thompson and his wife Catherine Lunham, died in Canada on 9 October 1861. [Chirnside gravestone, Berwickshire]

THOMSON, THOMAS, Second Lieutenant of the Royal Linlithgow Volunteers, was admitted as a burgess and guilds-brother of Dunfermline, Fife, on 15 August 1804. [DM]

THOMSON, WILLIAM, son of James Thomson a labourer in Common Close, Dalkeith, Midlothian, was accused of prison breaking in 1821. [NRS.AD14.21.220]

THORBURN, ADAM WILLIAM, in Clarendon, Jamaica, heir to her grand-uncle R. Thorburn or Thorbrand, a carrier in Hawick, Roxburghshire, in 1824. [NRS.S/H]

THORBURN, ALEXANDER, son of John Thorburn in Penicuik, Mid Lothian, died in New Orleans, Louisiana, in 1853. [S.16.7.1853]

THORBURN, GEORGE C., from New York, married Elizabeth Crawford, second daughter of William Crawford in Glasgow, in Earlston, Berwickshire, on 16 July 1819. [S.132.19]

THORBURN, GRANT, born 18 February 1773 in Dalkeith, Mid Lothian, son of James Thorburn a nail-maker, emigrated via Leith on board the Providence bound for New York in 1794, a nail-maker, writer and seedsman, died in Newhaven, Connecticut, on 21 January 1863. [ANY]

THORBURN, WILLIAM, born 1848, son of Robert Thorburn and his wife Mary, died at Waitangi, Chatham Island, New Zealand. [Coldingham gravestone, Berwickshire]

TOD, JAMES, and ANDREW TOD, grain merchants in Bo'ness, West Lothian, financial records from 1813 until1818. [NRS.CS96.107-118]

TOD, JOHN, son of John Tod in Goshen, Musselburgh, Mid Lothian, died in USA in 1853. [S.26.10.1853]

TODD, JOSEPH, born 1772, a merchant in North Berwick, East Lothian, emigrated to New York on the George of New York on 12 August 1807. [TNA.PC1.3790]

TOD, MARGARET, spouse of Reverend John Turnbull at Ayton, Berwickshire, testament, 1792, Comm. Lauder. [NRS]

TORRANCE, ARCHIBALD, jr., in Norwich, Connecticut, heir to his father Walter Torrance in Mullany, Currie, Mid Lothian, who died on 23 April 1848, 14 September 1900. [NRS.S/H]

TORRANCE, or SERVICE, ISABELLA, in Norwich, Connecticut, heir to her father Walter Torrance in Mullany, Currie, who died on 23 April 1848. [NRS.S/H]

TORRANCE, JOHN, in Norwich, Connecticut, heir to his father Walter Torrance in Mullany, Currie, who died on 23 April 1848, 14 September 1900. [NRS.S/H]

TRAIN, WILLIAM, a hatter in Kelso, Roxburghshire, was accused of reckless driving between Jedfoot Bridge and Crailing, in 1829. [NRS.AD14.29.216]

TROTTER, GEORGE, in Greenlaw, Berwickshire, testament, 1790, Comm. Lauder. [NRS]

TROTTER, ROBERT, a blacksmith in New York, later in Kelso, Roxburghshire, son and heir of John Trotter, a meal dealer in Kelso, in 1849. [NRS.S/H]

TROTTER, Reverend THOMAS, born 1782 in Lauder, Peebles-shire, was educated at Edinburgh University, a minister in Johnshaven, Kincardineshire, from 1808 until 1818, emigrated to Nova Scotia in 1818, a minister in Antigonish, N.S., from 1818 to 1853, died on 20 April 1855. [HPC] [UPC]

TUDHOPE, ROBERT, a skinner in Philadelphia, Pennsylvania, heir to his great grandfather Alexander Tudhope, a butcher in Selkirk, in 1837; also, heir to his grandfather Robert Tudhope, a butcher in Selkirk, in 1836. [NRS.S/H]

TULLOCH, MARGARET HELEN, born 1795, daughter of Thomas Tulloch of Elliston, Roxburghshire, died in Rome on 20 February 1874, an inventory, 1874. [NRS.SC70.167.881] [Protestant Cemetery, Rome]

TULLOH, THOMAS, in Barrackpore, India, son and heir of Robert Henry Tulloh of Ellieston, Roxburghshire, who died on 22 December 1853. [NRS.S/H]

TURNBULL, GAVIN, born 1765 in Berwickshire, a teacher in Charleston, South Carolina, was naturalised there on 23vOctober 1813. [NARA.M1183.1]

TURNBULL, GEORGE, eldest son of Robert Turnbull tenant in Softlaw, Roxburghshire, heir to his uncle James Turnbull, 4 May 1792. [NRS.S/H]

TURNBULL, GEORGE, born 1778, son of John Turnbull and his wife Alison Hunter in Wedderburn, Berwickshire, died in St Domingo in 1798. [Buncle gravestone, Berwickshire]

TURNBULL, JAMES, a sawyer in Dunbar, East Lothian, was accused of theft in 1818. [NRS.AD14.18.115]

TURNBULL, JAMES, born 1828, son of Thomas Turnbull and his wife Mary, died in Cairo, Egypt, on 15 February 1864. [Dalkeith gravestone, Mid Lothian]

TURNBULL, ROBERT WILSON, youngest son of James Walter Turnbull, a draper in Jedburgh, Roxburghshire, died in New York on 5 January 1840. [EEC.20014]

TURNBULL, Reverend WALTER, born 30 April 1817 in Hawick, Roxburghshire, settled at Mount Zion, St James, Jamaica, on 16 August 1849, died there on 16 March 1850. [Mount Zion gravestone, Jamaica]

TURNBULL, WILLIAM, son and heir of Walter Turnbull of Rashiegrain, Roxburghshire, 11 August 1791. [NRS.S/H]

TURNER, ROBERT NICHOLSON, born 1808, son of Captain Robert Turner of the Royal Engineers, from Kelso, Roxburghshire, died in Tobago on 17 November 1840. [EEC.20172]

URE, JOHN, son of David Ure in Haddington, East Lothian, a house-carpenter in South Carolina, probate, 20 October 1797, S.C.

VAIR, JAMES, a weaver in Selkirk, son and heir of Thomas Vair portioner of Darnick, Roxburghshire, 1844. [NRS.S/H]

VEITCH, JAMES, a tenant in Whiteacres, Cockburnspath, Berwickshire, testament, 1792, Comm. Lauder. [NRS]

VEITCH, JAMES, son of James Veitch a farmer at Musselburgh, Mid Lothian, was apprenticed to John Howden a saddler and beltmaker in Edinburgh on 15 March 1792. [ERA]

VERT, Miss E. B., from Haddington, East Lothian, married Robert Tait, also from Haddington, a resident of Elisabethtown, North Carolina, in New York on 17 February 1855. [EEC.22710]

WALKER, ANDREW, born 1772 in Roxburghshire, died in St John, New Brunswick, on 12 December 1823. [CG.18.12.1823]

WALKER, HAY, a candlemaker in Haddington, East Lothian, a bond of caution for James Burn an architect in Haddington, in 1800. [NRS.CS271.384]

WALKER, JAMES, a butcher in Philadelphia, Pennsylvania, heir to his uncle John Walker a butcher in Bo'ness, West Lothian, who died on 7 January 1869. [NRS.S/H]

WALKER, JAMES, born 9 August 1838 in Legerwood, Berwickshire, son of Reverend John Hunter Walker, was educated at Edinburgh University, later a minister at Channelkirk, Berwickshire, from 1862 to 1885, then became a farmer in British Columbia. [F.2.148]

WALKER, ROBERT, born 1837, son of William Walker and his wife Janet Neill, died in Australia on 24 April 1896. [Birgham, Berwickshire, gravestone]

WALKER, THOMAS, a saddler from Dalkeith, Mid Lothian, with his mother Mrs Ann Walker, emigrated to America in 1795. [NRS.GD51.1.492]

WALKER, THOMAS, son of James Walker a shoemaker in Bathgate, West Lothian, was apprenticed to Alexander Davidson a merchant in Edinburgh on 8 October 1800. [ERA]

WALKER, THOMAS, son of Robert Walker and his wife Isabella Kerr, died in Trey, USA, on 9 February 1861. [Earlston gravestone, Berwickshire]

WALLACE, JAMES, in Barnet, USA, so and heir of John Wallace, a farmer in Threepwood, Roxburghshire, in 1842. [NRS.S/H]

WANLESS, ARCHIBALD, born 1798 in Roxburghshire, a saddler in Charleston, South Carolina, was naturalised there on 11 October 1834. [NARA.M1183.1]

WARRACH, JAMES, of Prestonpans, East Lothian, a deed dated 21 December 1809. [NRS.RD5.221.255]

WATERSTON, ROBERT, a merchant in Boston, New England, grandson and heir of Mary Tait, wife of Robert Cassie, a weaver in North Berwick, East Lothian, in 1847. [NRS.S/H]

WATHERSTON, JOHN, from Greenlaw, Berwickshire, later in Jamaica, died by 1808. [NRS.GD2.384]

WATSON, CHARLES, son of Charles Watson a brewer in Dalkeith, Mid Lothian, was apprenticed to John Charles a candlemaker in Edinburgh on 20 June 1799. [ERA]

WATSON, GEORGE, born 1815, son of James Watson a shoemaker in Allanton, Edrom, Berwickshire, accused of the murder of William Mack in Eyemouth, Berwickshire, 1833. [NRS.AD14.33.379]

WATSON, JAMES, was accused of culpable and furious driving a cart in Currie, Mid Lothian, in 1825. [NRS.AD14.25.36]

WATSON, JOHN, born in Musselburgh, Mid Lothian, in 1751, settled in Charleston, South Carolina, around 1782, died 10 December 1812. [St Michael's gravestone, Charleston]

WATSON, WILLIAM DICKSON, Deputy Assistant Commissary General, eldest son of Adam Watson in Dunbar, East Lothian, died in Barbados on 29 August 1816. [DPCA.744]

WATSON, WILLIAM, in New York, son and heir of Joseph Watson, a clothier in Chirnside, Berwickshire, later in New York, in 1845. [NRS.S/H]

WATSON, Captain WILLIAM, in America, son and heir of Isabel Dalgleish, widow of T. Watson of Shields, Peebles-shire, in 1848. [NRS.S/H]

WATSON, WILLIAM, a baker in London, Ontario, son and heir of John Watson in Polworth. Berwickshire, who died on 19 May 1873. [NRS.S/H]

WATT, JOHN, was accused of aiding the escape of Donald McCaul from Linlithgow Tolbooth, West Lothian, in 1822. [NRS.B48.16.6.4]

WATT, MARY, second daughter of John Watt, married Andrew Anderson MD, eldest son of James Anderson from Devoespoint, New York, at Dunsmore Lodge, Corstorphine, Midlothian, on 30 August 1816. [DPCA.736]

WAUCHOPE, Lieutenant Colonel, of the 20th Regiment of Foot, eldest son of Andrew Wauchope of Niddrie, Midlothian, died from wounds received on 2 August 1813. [SM.76.78]

WAUGH, JAMES, in the poorhouse near Chillicothe, Ross County, Ohio, brother and heir of John Waugh a feuar in Kelso, Roxburghshire, 1833. [NRS.S/H]

WAUGH, JOHN, born 179-, '21 years in Jamaica', died in Melrose, Roxburghshire, on 27 December 1832. [Melrose gravestone]

WEATHERLY, JOHN, born 1819 in Cockburnspath, son of James Weatherly and his wife Janet, died in Fulham, Balmoral, Australia, on 7 September 1880. [Cockburnspath gravestone, Berwickshire]

WEDDERBURN, JOHN, born 18 August 1776 in Inveresk, East Lothian, eldest son of James Wedderburn, was educated at Glasgow University in 1789, emigrated to Jamaica in 1794, died there on 19 May 1799. [GC.1241][MAGU.157]

WEIR, ELIZABETH MOFFAT, daughter of A. Weir, a surgeon in Jamaica, cousin and heir of William Hunter in Swintonhill, Berwickshire, in 1810. [NRS.S/H]

WEIR, GEORGE, of Kames, a Lieutenant of the 32nd Regiment of Foot, 'who was barbarously killed by the rebels' at St Denis, Lower Canada, on 23 November 1837. [Eccles gravestone, Berwickshire]

WEIR, ROBERT COSENS, of Bogangreen, born 1840, Captain of the 1st Royals, died at Nussarabad, India, on 3 September 1867, husband of Caroline L. A. Irwin. [Eccles gravestone, Berwickshire]

WEIR, Dr WILLIAM, born 1812, eldest son of Dr Weir in Dunluce, Roxburghshire, died in Montpelier, Clarendon, Jamaica, on 17 November 1841. [AJ.4909]

WELLS, Mrs ANN, a seaman's widow in Bo'ness, West Lothian, a letter re a petition to Trinity House, London, 1840. [NRS.GD75.596]

WELSH, MARION, versus her husband John McCrie, a writer in Dunbar, East Lothian, a divorce in 1806. [NRS.CC8.6.1280]

WESTON, ALICE ANNE, youngest child of Dr Paul Weston in Charleston, South Carolina, was married in Portobello, Midlothian, to Edward Mahon Roose, son of Sir David Rose, on 29 April 1842. [EEC.20357]

WESTON, MARY ANN MAZYCK, second daughter of Dr Paul Weston in Charleston, South Carolina, was married in Portobello, Midlothian, to John Gibson, a Writer to the Signet, on 10 April 1849. [EEC.20357]

WHALE, ANDREW, a tailor in London, heir to his brother Lancelot Whale, Rector of Kelso Grammar School, Roxburghshire, 1793; also, to his nephew Robert Whale, only son of Lancelot Whale aforesaid, 2 September 1794. [NRS.S/H]

WHELPS, EUGENE AUGUSTUS, was accused of assaulting an officer of the law in High Street, Dunbar, East Lothian, in 1842. [NRS.AD14 28]

WHITE, ALEXANDER CHARLES, in Woodbine, Kansas, son and heir of James White, a tenant farmer on Ayton Law, Berwickshire, who died on 14 January 1858. [NRS.S/H]

WHITE, DAVID, Rector of Duns Grammar School, died on 19 August 1822. [SM.90.520]

WHITE, JAMES, born 1792 in Penicuik, a sawyer, was accused of discharging a firearm and wounding in Penicuik, Midlothian, in 1832. [NRS.AD14.32.384]

WHITE, MARGARET, in Brooklyn, New York, grand-daughter and heir of John White, a portioner in Duns, Berwickshire, in 1856. [NRS.S/H]

WHITE, THOMAS, a baker in North Berwick, East Lothian, was accused of forgery and uttering a forged bond in Haddington, East Lothian, in 1840. [NRS.AD14.40.319]

WHITE, THOMAS, a baker in Brooklyn, New York, grandson and heir of John White, a portioner in Duns, Berwickshire, in 1856. [NRS.S/H]

WHITE, WILLIAM, born 1780, son of David White, [1761-1822], schoolmaster at Duns, Berwickshire, and his wife Mary Johnston, [1743-1798], died in Virginia on 18 October 1814. [Duns gravestone]

WHITE, WILLIAM, a mariner at Tweedmouth, testament, 1820, Comm. Edinburgh. [NRS]

WHITEFORD, JOHN, born 1820 in Fala Blackshiels, Peebles-shire, died in Porto Plato, St Domingo, on 19 November 1861. [AJ.5953] [EEC.23682] [S.2071]

WHITEHEAD, JANE, daughter of George Whitehead a tenant in Lochrig, widow of George Hall tenant in Houndridge, Ednam, who died 17 April 1844, 1845. [NRS.S/H]

WHITELAW, THOMAS, born 1 October 1791, a surgeon in the Royal Artillery, died in Barbados on 22 October 1849. [Musselburgh gravestone, Midlothian]

WHYTE, DANIEL, a millwright in Tortula, second son of Reverend Thomas Whyte in Libberton, appointed his brother Wallace Douglas Whyte, a gentleman in Libberton, as his attorney on 8 May 1790. [NRS.RD2.252.1038]

WHYTE, GORDON, a millwright in Jamaica, third son of Reverend Thomas Whyte in Libberton, appointed James Marshall in Edinburgh as his attorney on 3 June 1790. [NRS.RD2.249.1059]

WHITLIE, JOHN, born 1800, son of James Whitlie, [1757-1845], a feuar in Ayton, and his wife Isabel Clark, died in South Trenton, New Jersey, on 30 April 1847. [Ayton gravestone, Berwickshire]

WILD, JAMES, son of John Wild a merchant in Penicuik, Mid Lothian, was apprenticed to John Watt a merchant in Edinburgh on 3 May 1794. [ERA]

WILKIE, JOHN, born 1838 in Peebles, died in Vancouver, British Columbia, on 28 November 1871. [St Andrew's gravestone, Peebles]

WILLIAMS, JOHN, born 1827 in America, a labourer in Wiselaw Mill, Lauder, accused of the murder and robbery of Andrew Mather at Cleekhimin Toll Bar in 1853. [NRS.JC26.1853.455]

WILLIAMSON, JOHN, a mulatto in Dunbar, East Lothian, was accused of rioting in Dunbar in 1816. [NRS.SC40.54.1.32]

WILLIAMSON, ROBERT, a mason in New York, son and heir of James Williamson, a mason in Gattonside, Roxburghshire, in 1848. [NRS.S/H]

WILSON, ALEXANDER, late of Gibraltar, died in Kelso, Roxburghshire, on 1 December 1815. [SM.77.77]

WILSON, HARRY, at Linlithgow Bridge, West Lothian, was accused of robbery in 1823, a petition. [NRS.B48.16.6.4]

WILSON, JAMES, a manufacturer in Earlston, Berwickshire, father of Robert Smith Wilson, who died in Havanna, Cuba, in April 1873. [S.9315]

WILSON, JOHN, from Duns, Berwickshire, a surgeon in the Royal Navy, in 1792. [NRS.S/H]

WILSON, JOHN, in Berwick, later in Oskawa, Canada, heir to his grand-aunt Margaret Wilson, wife of Adam Gibson, a watchmaker in Duns, Berwickshire, in 1851. [NRS.S/H]

WILSON, JOHN RUSSELL, born 1809, a baker, son of John Wilson a miller in Grangemouth, West Lothian, died in Halifax, Nova Scotia, on 21 September 1873. [GH.10547]

WILSON, JOHN, son of Thomas Wilson, [1806-1875], and his wife Elizabeth Ramage, [1810-1873], died in Corowa, Victoria, Australia, on 27 January 1902. [Lauder gravestone, Berwickshire]

WILSON, JOHN HISLOP, born 14 February 1849, son of Robert Wlson and his wife Janet ....., died in Auckland, New Zealand, on 5 December 1871. [Preston gravestone, Berwickshire]

WILSON, MARGARET, in Kelso, Roxburghshire, widow of Andrew Swanston a tailor in Kelso, heir to her father William Wilson a wright in Kelso, 1845. [NRS.S/H]

WILSON, MARGARET, in Belhaven, East Lothian, sister of Peter Wilson a surgeon in New Zealand, 1859. [NRS.S/H]

WILSON, PATRICK, agent in Kelso, Roxburghshire, for the British Linen Company in 1849. [POD]

WILSON, ROBERT, son of Robert Wilson a journeyman skinner in Dalkeith, was apprenticed to John Douglas a hatter in Edinburgh on 17 October 1799. [ERA]

WILSON, ROBERT, in Cincinatti, Ohio, nephew and heir of Betty Wilson, a dressmaker in Temple, Dalkeith, Midlothian, who died on 17 April 1854. [NRS.S/H]

WILSON, THOMAS, a canal labourer in Broxburn, West Lothian, was accused of prison breaking, in 1820. [NRS.AD14.20.258]

WILSON, THOMAS, born 1763, son of Robert Wilson, [1737-1782], and his wife Alison Darling, died in Philadelphia, Pennsylvania, on 26 January 1830. [Preston gravestone]

WILSON, WILLIAM, an ironmaster in Kinneil, West Lothian, died 24 September 1862, uncle of John Wilson in Tours, France. [NRS.S/H]

WINTER, WILLIAM, born 1789, son of William Wilson, 1734-1799], a wright in Greenlaw, and his wife Fanny Paterson, [1753-1830], died in Fort Augusta, Jamaica, on 23 December 1825. [Polwarth gravestone, Berwickshire]

WITHERSPOON, JOHN, born in Gifford, Haddington, East Lothian, on 5 February 1722, son of Reverend James Witherspoon minister of Yester, was educated at Edinburgh University in 1739, minister of the Laigh Kirk in Paisley, President of Princeton University, New Jersey, in 1768, signed the Declaration of Independence, died in 1794 in Princeton. [ANY][F]

WOOD, DAVID, a skipper in Dunbar, East Lothian, testament, 1826, Comm. Edinburgh. [NRS]

WOOD, GIDEON, a labourer in Ryestubble, Garvald Mains, East Lothian, was accused of poaching in 1827. [NRS.AD14.27.29]

WOOD, ROBERT, a skipper in Dunbar, East Lothian, testament, 1826, Comm. Edinburgh. [NRS]

WRIGHT, GEORGE, in Salton, East Lothian, applied to settle in Canada on 4 March 1815. [NRS.RH9]

WRIGHT, JOHN, son of Robert Wright a baker in Haddington, East Lothian, was apprenticed to a merchant in Edinburgh on 5 December 1791. [ERA]

WYLIE, JOHN, a farmer in Glover, Orleans County, North America, nephew and heir of Thomas Morrison, a chandler in Whitburn, West Lothian, who died on 17 December 1853. [NRS.S/H]

YAIR, ARCHIBALD MCDOUGALL, born in Eckford, Roxburghshire, son of Reverend Joseph Yair and his wife Helen McDougall, a Customs House officer in New York, died 6 July 1909. [F.2.111]

YAIR, JOSEPH, born 20 January 1840 in Eckford, Roxburghshire, son of Reverend Joseph Yair and his wife Helen McDougall, an accountant in Canada. [F.2.111]

YARREL, ELIZABETH, wife of Captain Yarrel in North Carolina, heir to his grand-uncle W. Begbie of Gifford Vale, East Lothian, in 1827. [NRS.S/H]

YORKSTON, ALEXANDER, a shoemaker in Linlithgow, West Lothian, was accused of robbery in 1823, a petition. [NRS.B48.16.6.4]

YORSTON, ALEXANDER, a labourer in Linlithgow, West Lothian, was accused of stealing beef in 1825. [NRS.B48.16.6.6]

YORSTON, ARCHIBALD, born 1779, sergeant of the Dalkeith Troop of the Royal Mid Lothian Yeomanry, died in January 1824. [Eddleston gravestone, Peebles-shire]

YOUNG, ALEXANDER, a mug selling tinker in Pathhead of Cranston, Mid Lothian, was accused of assault and wounding in 1819. [NRS.AD14.19.202]

YOUNG, ANDREW, a mug selling tinker in Dunbar, East Lothian, was accused of assault and wounding in 1819. [NRS.AD14.19.202]

YOUNG, GEORGE, a stockbroker in USA, grandson and heir of James Scott, a wright in Kelso, Roxburghshire, in 1854. [NRS.S/H]

YOUNG, HELEN CLARKE, in America, daughter and heir of James Young in Lilliesleaf, Roxburghshire, later in Edinburgh, in 1848. [NRS.S/H]

YOUNG, JAMES, born 1799, son of James Young, [1742-1784], died in Richmond, Virginia, on 2 August 1815. [Uphall gravestone, West Lothian]

YOUNG, JAMES, a feuar in Yetholm, Roxburghshire, a bond of caution, 1803. [NRS.CS271.847]

YOUNG, JAMES, born 1799, son of James Young, [1742-1784], died in Richmond, Virginia, on 2 August 1815. [Uphall gravestone, West Lothian]

YOUNG, JAMES HUME, born 11 October 1819 in Eckford, Roxburghshire, son of Reverend James Young and his wife Marion Hume, a missionary in Amoy, China, died in Musselburgh, Mid Lothian, in February 1855. [F.2.111]

YOUNG, JOHN, a mug selling tinker in Yetholm, Roxburghshire, was accused of assault and wounding in 1819. [NRS.AD14.19.202]

YOUNG, JOHN, a quarryman in Swineburn, Kirkliston, West Lothian, was accused of night poaching with an offensive weapon there, in 1830. [NRS.AD14.30.260]

YOUNG, JOHN, a mason in Lilliesleaf, Roxburghshire, son and heir of Peter Young a labourer there, 1841. [NRS.S/H]

YOUNG, ROBERT, a mug selling tinker in Kelso, Roxburghshire, was accused of assault and wounding in 1819. [NRS.AD14.19.202]

YOUNG, SAMUEL, a manufacturer in Dalkeith, Mid Lothian, sederunt book, 1809-1829. [NRS.CS96.921]

YOUNG, THOMAS, born 1734 in Dalmeny, Queensferry, West Lothian, a planter in Savannah, Georgia, died 7 November 1808, probate 14 November 1808, Chatham County, Georgia. [Georgia gravestone] [Savannah Death Register]

YOUNG, THOMAS, son of Archibald Young a farmer in Ingliston, Mid Lothian, died in New York on 1 September 1844. [EEC.210931]

YOUNG, WILLIAM, a feuar in Yetholm, Roxburghshire, a bond of caution, 1803. [NRS.CS271.847]

YOUNG, WILLIAM, born 1800 in Uphall, West Lothian, son of James Young, [1742-1784], died in Trelawney, Cornwall, Jamaica, in 1815. [NRS.RH1.2.804/1] [Uphall gravestone]

YULE, ARCHIBALD, late of the Dumfries Militia, applied to settle in Canada on 2 May 1827. [TNA.CO384.16.1E]

YULE, GEORGE, a wright in Haddington, East Lothian, was admitted as a burgess of Dunfermline on 4 June 1788. [DM]

CPSIA information can be obtained
at www.ICGtesting.com
Printed in the USA
JSHW012147130423
40285JS00006BB/177